We'll Be the Last Ones
to Let You Down

WE'LL BE
THE LAST ONES
TO LET
YOU DOWN

*Memoir of a
Gravedigger's
Daughter*

RACHAEL HANEL

University of Minnesota Press

MINNEAPOLIS

LONDON

Portions of chapters 1, 2, 11, and 13 were published in "We'll Be the Last Ones to Let You Down," *Bellingham Review* (Spring 2007). Portions of chapter 2 appeared in "Off the Beaten Career Path," *Ghoti* magazine (Labor Day 2007), www.ghotimag.com. Chapter 5 includes a version of "The First Glimpse," originally published in *Stardust and Fate: The Blueroad Reader* (Janesville, Minn.: Blueroad Press, 2007). Portions of chapters 6 and 12 appeared in "Break the Plow," *New Delta Review* (Spring 2011). Portions of chapter 8 were published as "Dad Digs Uncle Davey's Grave," *The Truth about the Fact: International Journal of Literary Nonfiction* (Spring 2009).

Published by the University of Minnesota Press
111 Third Avenue South, Suite 290
Minneapolis, MN 55401-2520
http://www.upress.umn.edu

ISBN 978-0-8166-8346-8 (pb)

A Cataloging-in-Publication record for this book is available from the Library of Congress.

Printed in the United States of America on acid-free paper

The University of Minnesota is an equal-opportunity educator and employer.

20   19   18   17   16   15   14   10   9   8   7   6   5   4   3

To Dad, of course
To Mom, for the stories

Precious in the sight of the Lord is the death
of his saints.

PSALM 116:15

CONTENTS

My parents' gravestone in Woodville Cemetery, Waseca,
Minnesota

Chapter 1

WE'LL BE THE LAST ONES
TO LET YOU DOWN

*I*GREW UP IN CEMETERIES. My summers weren't like the ones that other kids lived. My friends played in Waseca's parks on playground sets or swatted baseballs around diamonds or swam near Clear Lake's sandy beach. Instead, I ran around the necropolis, the city of the dead, taking in the fresh air, living and breathing and laughing as those below me no longer could. Spending so much time in cemeteries didn't bother me. I was there simply because that's where my parents' jobs brought me.

Dad and Mom made a living from people's inability to keep on living.

Dad controlled a gravedigging monopoly in and around Waseca, a small town in the middle of south-central Minnesota's fertile plains. He carved holes out of the earth in about twenty different cemeteries, burying bodies and dreams from Janesville to Medford, from Waldorf to Blooming Grove, burying farmers and accountants, teachers and mechanics, teenagers and parents, babies and grandparents.

Dad and Mom also mowed cemeteries. My older siblings, Renee and Andy, helped when not in school. I trailed Renee by nine years, Andy by seven, a gap large enough to make me feel like an only child at times. No one needed me for important jobs, such as running a lawnmower or helping Dad heave laden shovelfuls of dirt from the ground.

So I wandered.

Cemeteries fed my imagination, and looking back, they even gave birth to it. I was not yet three when Dad became a gravedigger. Just as our farmer neighbors coaxed the soil each year to bring forth life, I, too, cultivated my landscape, coaxing stories from the cemeteries to create my own definition of death.

THE ROOM I SHARED WITH RENEE looked less like a bedroom than a classroom. A big dry-erase board leaned against a wall, and in one corner sat a small school desk with an attached swivel chair that Mom and Dad had bought for me at a garage sale, so eager was I to start school. Many afternoons, after the bus dropped off Renee and Andy at the end of our gravel driveway, I sat at the desk watching Renee write colorful, loopy letters on the board with squeaky markers. I learned my letters, really learned them; I didn't just recite them like a parrot.

I devoured Dr. Seuss: *Hop on Pop, Fox in Socks, Cat in the Hat.* I didn't care that crayon and pen scribbles from Renee's and Andy's younger days marred the books. I didn't mind that they had printed their names in big block letters on inside front covers; I added mine there, too.

The books went with me to the cemetery. I read them cover to cover, over and over, as I sat in the truck while Mom mowed and Dad trimmed. Under my fingertips, the pages felt smooth and pulpy and smelled slightly moldy after years of use and then storage in dark closets.

Growing restless in the truck, I would hop out and glide among the gravestones. Letters of the alphabet grew on monuments, waiting for me to pluck and arrange them like flowers. I kept the dead alive as I recited the tangled and thick German and Polish surnames—Mittelsteadt, Ignaszewski, Schiefelbein. And when words came together, stories emerged like shimmery desert oases.

The stories crystallized once I learned math. My cousin Julie tagged along with us to cemeteries when her parents, Rosanne and Wayne, spent long summer days in their fields or tended to their dairy herd. Julie was four years older than I and eager to show off her newfound math skills about the same time I started to read. I followed her one day as we walked around Woodville, the whirring of the mowers at our backs. We stopped at the huge Augenbaugh monument, solid marble, framed by a canopy of evergreen branches. The footstones rested in a neat semicircle at the base of the headstone, each member of the family with his or her own small marker. I bent down to read the names.

"I wonder how old they were," I said.

"That's easy," said Julie, sinking to her knees. "You just subtract the year of birth from the year of death." I watched as she scratched invisible numbers in the air. "This woman was eighty-two when she died." I made Julie do it again and again, and the dash between birth and death dates breathed forth a life. The buried ceased being the dead and walked across the stage to tell their stories. A Midwestern *Our Town*, brought to life.

Books and gravestones are composed of not only mere letters. A book cannot exist by itself; it is mere ornamentation, just a pretty prop on a bookshelf or coffee table. A reader needs to come along and make meaning from it. From a distance, our

tombstones, too, function as mere ornamentation, escaping notice as we drive quickly past cemetery gates. But come close,
stop, really read, and the stories will speak to you.

I WAS ELEVEN YEARS OLD when Dad and Mom bought their
tombstone. It didn't strike me as unusual that Dad, at forty-
two, and Mom, at forty-one, had a gravestone, just as it didn't
strike me as unusual that Dad was a gravedigger. My parents
would die, I knew, with or without a gravestone.

Nothing so large had been installed in Woodville in more
than one hundred years, but I remember nothing of the day it
came through Woodville's gates, past the vault, the outhouse,
the mausoleum, down the hill to the northeast corner. It might
have arrived on a weekday, while I studied in school. Or it
might have been a weekend day, and I stayed home while Mom
and Dad went to the cemetery. Was it spring? Summer? Fall?

But when I finally saw it, its size and color struck me silent.
I touched the jet-black granite, warmed by the sun. Even reaching up with my arm as high as I could, a good two feet remained
out of my grasp. The ebony was so new and polished that I
could see my reflection. The white lettering popped against the
inky background. It was tall and skinny, like a forceful exclamation mark rising out of the ground.

Only small gravestones—just a couple of feet high, either
plain bluish-gray or dull red, the most inexpensive granite you
could buy—punctuated that corner of Woodville. Here rested
those farmers and accountants and teachers and mechanics
who had lived through the Depression, their monuments a tes-
tament to penny-pinching ways. Simple scripts with only the
basic information—names, birth dates, death dates. People here
didn't talk much about themselves, didn't give too much away;

that was for others to do. They didn't wear their hearts on their sleeves. You saw hearts only on gravestones, or on statues of Jesus and Mary, their fingers pointing lightly to their bleeding cores.

DAD NEEDED THE GRAVESTONE much sooner than anyone expected. He was dead too quickly to dig his own grave, as he always said he would have liked to do. Four years after the gravestone was erected, he entered the hospital in extreme pain. He was diagnosed with cancer one day and gone the next.

Just days before, I was with him at Woodville, picking up sticks in front of the lawnmower's path, tending flowers, watering sod. That was the last summer I spent in cemeteries. No more eating brown-bag lunches with Mom and Dad, resting on sun-warmed granite like salamanders, feeling the burn beneath our legs. No more gliding over blacktop and gravel roads on my three-speed bike that Dad hoisted into the back of the pickup alongside his sod cutter and shovels. No more riding endlessly among gravestones, wind drifting through my dishwater-blond hair, skinny legs pumping hard, blood coursing through my veins.

That was the last time my family was complete.

I knew death, and I thought that Dad's job would prepare me for the inevitable fact that one day he would die. I knew that people died young and tragically. I could recite such names in seconds—Eric Keller, Wanda Sell, Vicki Mittelsteadt, Brad Battenfeld. I knew that those left behind cried at the graveside. Like a theatergoer, over the years I watched a parade of mourners enter my field of vision at the cemetery, stay for a while on stage, then exit, retreating and fading. But after they departed the cemetery, then what? That's what I didn't know, what all those years in the cemetery couldn't teach me. What would happen after death's arms reached out to touch my family?

I didn't know, couldn't know, how his death would change us. Without him, we collapsed as a family unit. It became almost painful for Mom and Renee and Andy and me to be together because the hole was so obvious. In a family that was once eager to tell the stories of others, to speak their secrets, silence ruled. After Dad died, we barely spoke his name.

No one spoke of these things, not where I lived. We who were rooted here came from stoic Germans and Scandinavians, reserved northern Europeans who wore stony faces for the world while inside they withered. Tears were for closed doors only. Still waters run deep.

MY NAME IS ON THAT GRAVESTONE, on the back, the last branch of a sprawling family tree. The branches flow down and out— great-grandparents, grandparents, parents, then me. I'm tethered not only to the names written in stone but to their stories, too. The story of my life is bound up in the story of my parents, their life in the cemetery. It's bound up in the story of my grandparents and the grief they endured, of which I knew little until later in life. It's bound up in the stories of familiar strangers, people I never met but to whom I felt connected just by studying their gravestones over the years. The words, the stories, stretched into the distance, like Dorothy's yellow brick road: everything she needed to know was within her the entire time, but she needed to embark on a journey in order to find it and needed others to help her along the way.

In this black granite is a story, a story waiting for someone to put the letters together to form words, sentences, paragraphs, chapters.

Dad's graduation portrait, Southern School of Agriculture, Waseca, 1962
Mom's graduation portrait, Sacred Heart High School, Waseca, 1962

Chapter 2

DIGGER O'DELL

$\mathcal{I}$T IS A SUMMER EVENING on Waseca's Main Street. Dad is driving our 1979 powder-blue Cadillac, guiding the wheel loosely with his right hand, holding a cigarette between the two fingers of his left hand, and occasionally flicking ash out the window. Mom is in the front seat, us three kids in the back. As the youngest, I'm sandwiched between Andy and Renee on the white, buttery-smooth leather seat. Dad drives south on Main Street, approaching the town's only stoplight. We're headed toward the Yellow Mushroom restaurant for a couple of thin-crust pepperoni pizzas and root beer.

Half a block from the stoplight, an old woman gingerly steps off the curb and into the street. People jaywalk here all the time. I have no idea that in big cities this is considered illegal. The woman wears a plastic bonnet to defend her curls against the battling wind. Enormous sunglasses swallow the top half of her face. Loose nylons gap on her legs, and her dress flitters in the breeze. She's one woman, yet she's every old woman I've ever met.

She steps into the path of the Cadillac. This is also common. Old people here have more faith that cars will stop for them than they have in Jesus Christ.

Dad hits the brakes. But he says, looking back at us in the rearview mirror, eyes dancing. "Business has been a little slow. Should I gun it?"

Dad dug more than one hundred graves a year. Death didn't deliver the bodies neatly spaced, one every three days. Instead, they came in bunches—ten or so in a two-week period, then two weeks with nothing. This was one of those nothing periods.

I laugh at Dad's joke, and so do Renee and Andy. I picture the absurdity of running over an old woman and giggle uncontrollably. Mom shoots Dad a sharp look, says, "Geez, Paul!" but she smiles, too.

He presses the gas pedal with his foot, and we speed forward a few feet. Dad stops well short of the woman, and we laugh even harder. He repeats this joke many times throughout the years. It never gets old.

DAD GOES TO WORK EARLY ALWAYS, so early that it's still dark. Maybe it's his genetics, growing up with a farmer dad who passed down a predetermined sleep pattern through DNA. Or maybe it's a throwback to before electricity and alarm clocks, when those who worked the land abided by primal circadian rhythms. Or maybe it's simply the mass quantities of caffeine and nicotine that he consumes, a constant buzz flowing through his veins, making him restless and jittery all the time. In any case, when I awaken, all that's left of him is a cooling coffeepot and lingering cigarette smoke. On clear summer days, he pulls out from our gravel driveway onto the blacktop road just as the sun, a shimmering red half circle, stretches out of its horizon bed. He needs to beat the humid heat that later will swell.

He most often starts the day in Waseca at Woodville, his biggest cemetery. He drives the eight miles from our house into town, makes a series of turns, and takes the blacktop road that heads east out of town. Railroad tracks run parallel to his right, guiding trains that make stops in Owatonna, Rochester, Chicago, to dump coal and grain.

Just on the edge of town, Dad slows the truck and turns left into Woodville Cemetery. We bury our dead on the outskirts of the city. Only a couple of houses border the fence. The cemetery is on a knoll, above a marsh on which nothing can be built. To the east and south are only cornfields and soybean fields.

When Dad turns, shovels rattle against the sod cutter in the back and the steel of the truck bed. The backhoe, sitting atop a trailer, sways and lurches with every bump, but the strong chain keeps it firmly anchored. In the truck, the voices of Charlie Boone and Roger Erickson on WCCO-AM grow softer as Dad turns down the radio knob.

He winds his way past the brick vault. That's where bodies are stored over the winter. Most burials are halted throughout the harsh Minnesota winter. It is difficult to dig a grave when the ground is frozen solid for two, sometimes three, feet down. The caskets and the bodies within them accumulate through April, when the soil finally thaws and green buds pop on the trees. Dad is real busy then, sometimes having to bury twenty-some people over the course of just a few days. He works those days at warp speed. Everything seems to move in fast motion, his arms and legs like hummingbird wings. By June, though, after the rush of spring burials and trying to make the cemeteries perfect for Memorial Day, his life runs in real time.

Dad rolls down his window, turning the crank with his left hand. He draws into his lungs sweet air—a mixture of crops, dew, petunias, dirt. To him, nothing smells quite this good. Not soap, not his Old Spice, not our wood-burning stove. He waited years to work in fresh air. For fourteen years, from right after high school until 1977, he slopped feed into hog troughs and cleaned manure off concrete floors using noxious chemicals that burned his nose. For fourteen years he came home reeking of pig.

The truck heads straight for the "mozzy," what we call the mausoleum, the Parthenon-like structure around which lie Waseca's founding families, the Everetts and the Curtisses. Then Dad veers left and down a slight hill. In the still of the morning, Clear Lake is a mirror, seen through the row of evergreens that mark Woodville's northern edge. If Dad didn't have to work, he'd take out the boat and catch some sunnies. In the drought of '88, Dad and Mom and I fished for days on end. Groundskeeping slowed to a halt that summer as the sun transformed spongy cemetery grass into sharp pricks of brown.

At Woodville, Dad slows the truck, jiggles the stick shift into park, and shuts off the ignition. He climbs down from his seat; his heavy work boots meet grass. He reaches a long arm behind the pickup's seat—past a roll of paper towels, tools, garbage—and palms the smooth cardboard carton. Picking up the package, he tilts it downward, and a pack of cigarettes comes tumbling out. He grabs a matchbook from the dashboard, lights the cigarette, takes that first inhale, and coughs. Phlegm rises from his lungs, moves through his windpipe, and lands as a gob in his mouth. He turns his head and spits.

He continues puffing as he grasps the shovel and heavy sod cutter from the pickup bed. His thick forearms and biceps bulge against the weight as he carries the tools to the spot where he has to dig this morning. He eases the sod cutter into place, presses a heavy boot against a bottom ledge, and throws his 220 pounds against it. The blade slices through the grass and three inches of soil. It cuts a strip a little more than a foot wide. He does this three more times, rolls the strips into neat rounded curls, and sets them next to the headstone. The black scar on the ground is like a missing tooth.

He walks back to the truck and pulls out a piece of plywood. By the time he hauls it to the incipient grave, his breath comes in short, hurried gasps. He tries to breathe deeply, but it's as if his lungs are coated in cement. He sets the plywood on the grass next to the grave. Without it, the backhoe's weight would sink into the ground, kill the grass, and leave ugly tire tracks. He's not going to mess up his cemetery. He wants to leave no trace of himself. People have a right to come here and not have to look at ugly gashes in the grass. Walt Kinder, one of Waseca's funeral directors, likes to say visitors don't want to be reminded a grave was dug. Dad doesn't quite understand—how do they think bodies get into the ground?—but he plays along. So he sets a goal for himself at each grave: by the time he's finished, by the time the dead are in their resting places, the grave should look as though he hadn't been there. That shows he's done a good job. He likes to think people imagine the body magically buried itself.

Back at the truck, he places a pair of wood planks against the trailer's back lip and angles them down to the road. Tiny drops of sweat dance on his forehead. After taking off the chains that secure the backhoe, he pulls a small set of keys from his front pants pocket, fires the engine, maneuvers the backhoe from its perch, and backs down the planks. Reversing direction, he motors over to the grave.

The controls for the smaller digging claw sit high atop the backhoe, so he climbs to the top seat. There, he's a kid playing an arcade game, moving the claw forward, down, then back up with dirt in its mouth. Another hand movement swings the bucket to the right, where he plops dirt onto a second piece of plywood. He digs down roughly four-and-a-half feet. That will leave enough room between the top of the vault holding the coffin and the top of the grave once everything is in place.

The ground's gaping hole looks rough, imprecise. The small bucket is no fine sculptor. So he shuts off the ignition and lets nature sink into his ears. Nothing but the constant chirp of robins and sparrows and the lonesome cry of mourning doves. He feels as if he's breathing in through a damp washcloth, the air is so heavy. No doubt a thunderstorm will form later in the day. He draws a white handkerchief from his right pocket and wipes his brow. The sweat beads come faster and stronger. Each individual bead joins with its neighbor, like small creeks flowing together. Pretty soon he has the Mississippi running off his nose, even though it's only seven o'clock.

The shovel rests on the headstone; he takes it and lays it on the ground near the grave's edge. He descends into the hole. His head and shoulders rise above ground level. He likes this part, going down into the grave. The earth is cool. The coolness fans from the side walls, almost in waves, rhythmic like a breath, the earth itself a living being. He wields the shovel into the four corners, carving and smoothing dirt caked with roots. Earthworms wiggle in and out of their caves.

He stops. Closes his eyes. Thinks. Rests. He quiets all thoughts of what he's done and what he yet needs to do. He retreats, times his breath with the breath of the earth. He soaks in coolness, lets it spill over him.

God filters into his thoughts. Dad thinks how a body will go into this space in a few hours, that it's just a body, a shell, nothing more. The spirit will not rest here; instead, it will drift somewhere out there, above. He envisions heaven. He wonders if the spirit stays in one piece and floats up to St. Peter at the pearly gates to look down from above. Then he thinks maybe the spirit dissolves into a million pieces and descends gently onto everything in the world like a fine dust, that everything in the world holds an invisible layer of people who have died. Or maybe the spirit breaks into just enough pieces to stick to the places and people it loved most. He likes that thought best. When he goes, he'd like part of him to stick around here, this place, his space. This wouldn't be a bad spot in which to linger for eternity.

Time slows, stops. He's down there thinking for only a couple of minutes, but his mind moves across a lifetime. He's heard how people's entire lives flash before them in the instant before death. How could that be? What will he think about when his time comes?

TIME ANNOUNCED ITSELF in our house with great zeal. A grandfather clock firmly anchored our living room wall, Dad's limited edition eagle prints framing it on either side. The clock's three large, heavy weights glowed golden late afternoons when sunlight burst through our west-facing bay window.

The clock chimed every quarter hour, the four notes thick and resonant. Authoritative, rich "dongs" marked the top of each hour. The vibrations thrummed throughout the house even after the chimes had stopped.

At one point, we had three clocks in the living room: the grandfather clock, a smaller tabletop clock that also chimed on the quarter hour, and a Bavarian cuckoo clock that Renee brought home from Europe after her senior year of high school. For weeks, the three clocks marked time regularly, day and night. The cuckoo bird was particularly insistent, cawing every fifteen minutes. I slept heavily through the sounds, as did Dad. Mom, on the other hand, soon put the bird to sleep. At night she stopped the gears, and the bird stayed hidden in its house.

In the morning, she let him out again. But it wasn't long before she neglected to let him call out during the day, too. She left the chiming clocks alone, and they continued to proclaim the passage of time.

The notion of time, this thing that philosophers struggle to define, became concrete in our house. We could reach out and touch the cool brass of the clocks. It wasn't enough that we could see and feel time; we could hear it, too.

Dad worked with constant reminders of time, or more accurately, constant reminders that time runs out. He saw time, too, in the form of dates inscribed on gravestones. And for more than three years he faced his own gravestone, with the date that marked his beginning and the space that waited for an end date to follow, a reminder that his time, like everyone else's, would run out.

Perhaps this is why Dad became hyperaware of time, his senses fine-tuned to every passing second. We were never late. We arrived at Mass early. Dad drove me to band practices before school, and I was usually the first one there, delivered at least fifteen or twenty minutes early. I sometimes beat the band director and had to wait outside the school door until Mr. Brooks unlocked it with his key. Dad sold gravestones on the side, making evening prearrangement appointments with clients. He arrived early enough to sit in the car and have a cigarette before ringing the doorbell on time, his briefcase of granite samples firmly in hand. If snow hampered travel, then he left home extra early.

He dug graves well ahead of the funeral. He picked up the two local newspapers early in the morning, practically the moment they were distributed in the predawn to gas stations. He'd quickly turn to the obits page. Then he'd listened to KOWO-AM at 9:15 a.m. for the announcement of local obituaries. After that, he'd visit Walt Kinder or Dick Sandberg, Waseca's other funeral director, to see if there was anyone he had missed.

He'd arrive at the cemetery long before the graveside service. He'd check the grave to make sure that it hadn't caved in or that water hadn't seeped into the bottom. If something was wrong, arriving early gave him time to fix it. Arriving early also gave him time to find the perfect hiding spot so he would stay out of view of the mourners.

Dad carried a pocket watch. A wristwatch wouldn't have lasted long, not with all the mowing, trimming, and digging and the dirt and grass that went along with the work. The pocket watch was nothing fancy, no heirloom, just a trusty piece of metal that he had to wind. It was tarnished and dulled by his fingerprints after handling it dozens of times each day. After work, Dad would come through the door, walk into the kitchen, and empty the contents of his pockets on top of the refrigerator. And there the watch would sit until the next morning, when he would slip it into the shirt pocket of his dark-blue work shirt, never failing to mark the time.

THE GRANDFATHER CLOCK had just finished its twelfth bong. It was not the chimes that awakened me but the telephone. My stomach dropped at the sound and I stared into darkness. I'd watched enough movies and television shows to know that a ringing phone deep in the night never brings good news. From across the hall, I could hear Dad's low voice mumbling a hello. I pulled my pillow over my ears. Whatever the bad news was, I didn't want to hear it just then. I forced myself back to sleep.

When I woke up in the morning, I walked into the kitchen to pour a bowl of cereal. Mom was wiping the counter around the sink. Dad, wearing his work blues, sat at the dining room table, his chair sideways to the table so he was facing me and Mom in the kitchen.

"Neil died," he said.

Uncle Neil. Another of Dad's brothers. Another heart attack, at just fifty-three years old. Seven years earlier it was Uncle Davey, dead at forty-four.

I took my cereal bowl to the table and slid into a chair across from Dad. Because he was sitting sideways, I saw him in profile. His head was bowed, eyes turned to the floor. Dad's sadness was quiet, but deep, starting at the surface of the skin and sinking far into his bones. It sunk so far down that Dad couldn't fight it. It weighed him down, and his body slumped in the chair, feet stretched out before him. Dad was only forty-five years old, but on that morning I thought, for the first time, that he was starting to look old.

Some say that we can't see time, that it's an invisible fourth dimension. But we can see its evidence—the gears of a clock, the swing of a pendulum, the aging of a face. On this day, Dad's gray hair at his temples seemed to have crept farther back, and his crow's feet and laugh lines appeared a little deeper. I no longer saw the young dad from his graduation or wedding photos, the ones I studied with fascination, trying to imagine his life before me. I didn't even see the dad from more recent photos. Instead I glimpsed what he might look like at fifty-five or sixty-five. The drumbeat of death, always present around him, marched even closer, became more persistent. When would it be his time? What I saw at the table was a man contemplating his own mortality.

This was the first time I'd seen what the heaviness of time had inflicted on Dad. Surely there had been moments when he'd felt this before, when he buried people he knew, relatives or neighbors or children. I hadn't heard the snippets of conversation between him and Mom: *That's too bad* or *She was so*

young or *Those poor kids at home.* I had been too young to notice his nuanced changes in mood, the way he'd become quiet
and contemplative.

I sat there quietly, almost afraid that my breathing would
disturb this thing I was seeing, holding my breath as I did when
I saw a deer in the trees. For Dad, it was a rare show of emotion, a physical nod to time. But as soon as I got a glimpse of
this fragile being, it was gone. Dad stood up, took a deep breath,
and moved on. He had Neil's grave to dig.

DAD'S GRAVES GREW GREEN AND LUSH. In 1976, he had started
digging at small country cemeteries—St. Jarlath's, St. Mary's,
Medo—while still working as a farm laborer at the University
of Minnesota Southern Experiment Station. His careful ways—
how he covered his tracks, the way he filled five-gallon pails
with water to coax the sod of freshly dug graves back to life—
secured him the larger cemeteries and gave him a new role to
play.

When Dad quit the experiment station, he shed the name
Paul Hager like an ill-fitting suit. He morphed into Digger
O'Dell, taking the name from a character on the old *Life of
Riley* radio and television shows. He was like a Method actor.
He slid so easily into this character that if you believe in des-
tiny, you would have to believe it had been waiting for him
all along. From the moment he was born, he belonged in a
cemetery.

He ordered pens, playing cards, stationery, and baseball caps
stenciled with "Digger O'Dell" and his logo, a smiling, car-
toonish man with an exaggerated nose riding a backhoe. Dad
and Mom came up with the motto, "We'll be the last ones to
let you down," and had that stamped on everything, too. The
supplies were mailed to our house in large brown boxes. When

they arrived, Dad carried them to his basement office and opened them like a kid digging into gifts on Christmas morning. He passed them along to me for inspection. I slid caps off pens and scribbled on the stationery with thick, black lines. I took playing cards out of their boxes; they were so shiny and new that they slid out of my hands and fell to the floor. Dad stuffed these goodies into his truck so he'd always have a ready supply to hand out to friends, neighbors, funeral directors, waitresses.

For his pickup truck he ordered a bug shield lettered with "Digger O'Dell." People might not have known Dad, but they sure knew Digger O'Dell. Driving down country roads, Dad was constantly giving the two-finger "farmer wave"—left elbow casually resting on the door frame, right hand loosely guiding the wheel, index and middle fingers raised in salute to an oncoming vehicle.

He created a uniform of his own choosing, a costume for the stage. He walked the cemeteries in dark-blue, durable cotton pants and a short-sleeved shirt made of the same material. The sun imprinted a dark brownish-red triangle on the otherwise pale skin exposed by the shirt's V-neck and colored the skin on his arms not covered by sleeves.

Each spring, just before the grass turned green (it seemed to do so overnight), Dad would buy a pair of heavy Red Wing work boots for the season. The old pair from the previous year had hundreds of miles on them, a permanent coat of bright-green grass clippings that looked as if it had been spray-painted on, and holes in the toes.

His feet grew hard and tough from all the walking. At night, in front of the TV, he would lean forward in his recliner and take a scissors to his feet, cutting off calluses. The extra skin was at least a quarter-inch thick.

Dad sweated through his uniform each day, even in the cool of spring or fall. Grime collected underneath his fingernails and settled into the rough grooves of his hands. No amount of scrubbing could remove all the dirt. When he shook hands at Mass, or with other parents at my band concerts, he looked clean, but if you looked closely at his hands, some graveyard dirt was always there, under the fingernails, in the creases of his skin.

In the role of Digger O'Dell, Dad could confront death head-on, interact with it, share the stage with it. It was Digger O'Dell who jokingly threatened to run down old ladies on Waseca streets. It was Digger O'Dell who told old guys at church like Fred Harguth that he'd be digging their graves one day. It was Digger O'Dell who proclaimed, over and over, "We'll be the last ones to let you down." It was Digger who came home, stripped off the uniform, and washed away dirt and death in a shower in our entryway so he wouldn't bring the cemetery grime any farther into the house. It was Paul Hager who emerged from the shower. He placed his work clothes in the washer, which was nearby. When Mom and Dad remodeled our house in 1981, they made sure Dad could be clean before he stepped into the main house. In this place, in the sacred interior of the home, the holy of holies, death was not part of our conversation.

Digger O'Dell was distanced from death. In his stage that was a cemetery, the procession of mourners was a faceless chorus, the dead played the starring role, and Digger O'Dell and the vault guy were supporting characters. Even morticians, like Kinder or Sandberg, were called funeral "directors," orchestrating the whole show like a Jerome Robbins or Hal Prince. But try as he might, Dad could never shake off death. He could try to separate life and death, but they wound around him like a rope pulled tight. A piece of it always lingered, always came home with him and lived with us.

Dad and Mom's wedding, St. Mary's Catholic Church,
rural Waseca, June 6, 1964

Chapter 3

IN THE MIDST OF LIFE WE
ARE IN DEATH

OM GRADUATED FROM HIGH SCHOOL in the spring of 1962, like Dad. But unlike Dad, whose path could be easily traced from high school to work at the experiment station to marriage, Mom had a missing year between graduation and the fall of 1963, when she met Dad.

I asked her once about that year, when I was seven or eight. I stood next to her in the kitchen as she washed dishes.

"Mom, what did you do right after high school, before you met Dad?"

She paused a moment, then said crisply, "I went to college in Washington." She didn't look at me, just removed a dripping dish from the sudsy water.

Something about the way she said it—the way she didn't meet my eye, the tone of finality—suggested that I stop asking questions. But her comment didn't make sense to me. Washington? Why would she go to college halfway across the country? This was a woman who never went anywhere, a woman who had never left home. Except for that missing year, she had never lived more than a mile from a parent. All the while I was growing up, she could have thrown a rock out her kitchen window and hit her father's house.

And nothing about Grandma and Grandpa Zimny indicated that they valued a college education, especially at a college so far away. Mom's two brothers went into the army after high school, and her sister Margaret got married immediately after graduation and went to work. And if Mom indeed had gone to college, why just one year? It was almost as if that year had magically been erased, the years surrounding it simply stitched together to absorb it. The mystery only deepened after I asked Renee if she knew anything about this strange story, the story of Mom's one year of college.

Renee's head swung in my direction. "Don't ever ask Mom what she did after high school," she snapped. I bit my lip. Renee must have known something I didn't, some type of sordid secret about Mom. The admonition was enough to shut me up for years.

NOVEMBER 22, 1963. The young, charismatic president has just been shot. Their president. Smooth, charming, good-looking. Catholic, like them. A pall descends over the country, an eclipse changes daylight into darkness, hope into anxiety. A collective grief hangs like a veil over the eyes. But the grief is suspended for just a moment, as a young man and a young woman have a first date.

The man, nineteen years old, tall and thin, hair gelled into a ducktail, always smiling, a smile made goofy with a front left incisor chipped from a years-ago fight with a sister. Always a cigarette between two fingers of one hand. Always talking, won't shut up, won't stop joking, won't stop laughing. Those with little patience consider him obnoxious.

The woman, six days shy of nineteen, short and petite, dark

brown hair swept into a French roll, light-blue eyes peering through cat-eye glasses. Quiet, she lets the young man do all the talking. Always a cigarette between her fingers, too.

They do not succumb to the shadows the images cast. The queen on a plane weeps, still wearing her pink suit smeared with blood. Children are dazed; they will barely recall their father's embrace. The couple promised Camelot, and now it's over. What's next? There's a war in a place called Vietnam that's just beginning. Rumors of a draft swirl. The young man is at the perfect age to be taken, snatched away from his parents, from Waseca, from this petite young lady friend.

But tonight, a romance buds. The romance trumps everything and demands their attention. *In the midst of life we are in death,* says the Book of Common Prayer. But tonight, *in the midst of death we are in life.*

They begin to meld, but they don't know it. They begin to come together, but they can't see it. Pieces of their individual auras leap and jump like charged particles and land on each other. What's around them gets thrown into the mix, too. A whirlwind of particles whips around them, wispy strands of a nation's grief and mourning, unseen but just as real as the dancers, the musicians, the empty beer bottles on tables. A whirlwind that twirls as fast as the dancers, full of energy and movement and vitality, faster and faster with each drumbeat. The young man and woman laugh and spin, unaware of this new thing that's being created. A new couple forms from the mix, emerges from the primordial courtship. The nation's grief of this time will leave its imprint on them. Their parents have suffered, too, in their own ways, a genetic line of grief filtering down. If they only knew. They cannot fathom how well they will know death.

* * *

MOM AND DAD MARRIED THE FOLLOWING JUNE. Dad had just turned twenty; Mom was yet nineteen. They married at St. Mary's Catholic Church, Mom's home church in rural Waseca County. It was a classic white-with-a-steeple country church, the type that was mirrored in thousands of ways across the country. It sat atop a knoll, catching any little breeze and magnifying it. In the wedding pictures, Mom holds down her veil with a hand as her skirt billows around her. Across the road is a cemetery, where Mom's baby nephew is buried, where her mother and father later will lie under the ground.

In another photo, taken at the wedding reception, Mom and Dad sit at the head table, Father Kellen standing behind them, his hands on their shoulders. They appear absolutely petrified. The rush into a wedding was not unusual for that time or place.

Mom and Dad might have married quickly anyway, but the Vietnam War, consciously or unconsciously, sped up the matter. A draft deferment was more likely for a married man, a primary wage earner, and much more likely for a father. Renee was born fourteen months after the wedding. Just a couple of years later, when Mom gave birth to Andy, her little brother Ray would already be in the Vietnamese jungle.

IN FRENCH, *renée* means "one who is born again," derived from the Latin *renascentis*. Though the young parents know Latin in the context of pre–Vatican II masses, they decided on the name simply because they think it's a pretty name for a chubby baby with whorls of thick, dark hair. With an accent on the second syllable, a drawn-out, light "ehhhh," your mouth opens and can't help but form a slight smile. A happy name, a bit of the classics on the prairie.

The night of Renee's baptism, the early September air hangs thick. The crickets chirp a symphony. It's a clear night; the stars burn intensely bright out here in the country. Dad is outside, smoking a cigarette. He counts the number of cricket chirps in a minute to decipher the temperature. Warm yet, around eighty. He thinks about the baby inside the house. Warm excitement fills his belly. A baby, he thinks; he's a dad. He bought cigars with pink wrappers and delivered them to his brothers and friends. Today, his brother Neil and his wife, Donna, stood watch over the baby at the baptismal font. Mom and Dad chose Neil as godfather for their first baby. Neil is older by seven years, but he's the one out of seven brothers that Dad feels closest to. He doesn't know why. Dad just knows that in a big family some are more alike than others, and he and Neil think the same way, act the same way.

A blur in the corner of Dad's eye stops his reverie. It's a falling star. Not just any falling star, but one that blazes red, orange, and yellow, a star that streaks low, very low, and very close, across the eastern sky. He swears it lands behind the grain bin. He stands and looks out that way, but it's dark. The grain bin is a couple of hundred yards away. He thinks of walking back there. Wouldn't that be something, to find a chunk of meteor, something from outer space, right here on the farm? He takes a few steps forward, but something holds him back. Maybe it's the chills that crawl like cold fingers up his spine, raising the hairs on the back of his neck and leaving goose bumps on his arms. It's dark and quiet; the crickets have stopped chirping. He's not sure what he'll find, but he knows for certain it's from another world. He's seen one too many episodes of *The Twilight Zone*. He decides he prefers the mystery.

Dad waits a few more minutes to make sure all stays quiet, then he goes back into the house. He peers in on Renee, sleeping in her crib. He walks over and cradles her head with the back of his hand. His hand so big, her head so tiny. He thinks about the piece of heaven that fell.

Parts of one world crash into another. A baby crashes into this world, all red and wrinkled and startled. One day, she'll crash out of this world into the next, a glowing, fiery meteor transcending time and space.

THEY THOUGHT RAY WENT MIA in the jungle. Letters went unanswered. News of an attack on his platoon came back. A month went by, six weeks. Grandma and Grandpa steeled themselves. They told themselves that their youngest child was dead. A bookend of death, to match the death of their oldest, a stillborn, buried in an anonymous grave in a cemetery in their hometown an hour away. Ray would be buried at St. Mary's. Maybe then they would bring the baby here to join him, so he wouldn't feel so alone.

But Ray wasn't MIA. The word was slow to get back home. He was hurt, with shrapnel lodged beneath his skin. He spent weeks in a military hospital. He returned physically healed, but like so many vets he didn't speak of his time in 'Nam and would not, absolutely would not, ever eat rice again.

DAD GREW UP in the north part of Waseca County, Mom just south of center. The immigrant wanderings of three generations of Hagers and Zimnys stopped in Waseca County. Dad grew up in the 1950s in a township appropriately named Blooming Grove. It bloomed with corn and soybeans, prairie grasses and wildflowers. It took all of Grandma and Grandpa Hager's time and energy to keep their fourteen children fed and clothed and sheltered. There was no time to talk about who might have wanted to become a doctor or a lawyer or an astronaut. Even if there had been time to talk about it, there was no money to pursue it. Grandpa, with a country school education that stopped at eighth grade, provided for his family the only way he knew: he worked the land. It's what his father did before him, and his father before him, fathers going all the way back to Bohemia. Raising a farm family is what Grandma knew, with the stout and sturdy Hollinger and Liebing women before her working as farmwives and housewives and mothers all the way back to Alsace-Lorraine. My grandparents had no reference beyond farm life, and their children had no idea how they could even attempt to escape small-town living.

The Hager kids would have jobs, not careers. A job is a task, something done simply for pay. A job is not fulfilling. A job is where you punch in, do the work, and punch out at the end of the day. A career, though—a career is different. Even the very way the words sound: *job*—short, harsh, too much like *jab*, painful; but *career* flows off the tongue. "Career" comes from the Latin *carrus*, which can mean a swift course, like the way the sun moves across the sky. One of the dictionary definitions of "career" is also a swift course, the way one progresses through life. A career brings enjoyment, is closely intertwined with identity; it's who you are. It's not easy to separate career and life, whereas job and life have clearer delineations. In a career, you bring your skills and talents to the table—a career allows you to pursue them and use them to make money. In the Hager bunch, there may have been a kid with the potential to become a skilled graphic artist or musician or cardiologist. But it takes time and energy to pursue a career, knowledge of how to pursue it, and support. It's as if each generation could improve on itself only in baby steps. The Hager kids improved on what their parents had: each kid graduated from high school. To dream of college, to take that additional leap, would have been too much, too soon. After high school, the goal was to get a job, get married, and start a family. Their worlds were small. Whatever was beyond Blooming Grove Township, beyond south-central Minnesota, no one needed to know about it.

DAD GRADUATED from Waseca's Southern School of Agriculture in 1962, one of four "ag" high schools (when I was young, I thought Dad had gone to an "egg" school) scattered across Minnesota. Farm kids like Dad attended school only September through March, which allowed them to work the family fields during harvest and planting. They lived a quasi-college life, sleeping in dorms and going home on weekends. They learned not only reading, writing, and arithmetic but also plant genetics and butchering (for the guys), and sewing and home economics (for the girls). Dad, tall and wiry, played football and basketball. But he, and almost everyone else in his class of fifty-one, also participated in "artsy" activities like the class play and glee club.

The caption under Dad's senior photo says, "No excitement, I'll make some!" He's grinning wide, his hair shaped into the popular ducktail pompadour of the time. Something lurks behind that smile: a zest, a zinger, a mischievous streak. At least he wasn't stuck with a lame caption like some of his classmates. The yearbook staff must have struggled to come up with lines such as "He takes his responsibilities seriously" or "She makes good use of her extra time and study hours!" Those were probably the serious students who got As and went to college—students unlike Dad.

Dad's senior yearbook flows with good wishes and reminiscences, squeezed into every blank spot, written every which way in the front and back. When I was little, I pored over those pages until the seams fell apart, fascinated by Dad's life before he was "Dad." I turned the book upside down to decipher the girls' flowing scripts and the cramped scrawls of the boys.

To the riot of the dorm

Best wishes always to one of the goofiest guys I know

Here's to the loudest senior ever!

For heaven's sake behave now

Here's hoping the joker of our class will be as good in the world as he can be

To the only kid in school that can smoke and not get caught

Although you were indeed a very excellent convict in our class play, I really think you would make a better politician! Whatever your chosen profession is, Good Luck!

DAD'S OLDER BROTHERS, John, Neil, and Donnie, worked at Owatonna Tool Company, and when Dad graduated from the ag school they said, *It's a great place to work. Easy job, benefits. They have some openings. We could get you right in.* So Dad joined the hundreds of others there, waiting in line to punch the time clock, standing like sentries at machines watching parts go by, sitting at tables chowing down sandwiches and gulping coffee on half-hour lunch breaks. He felt like a lab rat, doing the same thing over and over for his reward. He went outside only for cigarette breaks; even those were dictated by the bosses. He tried to suck down as many cigarettes as he could in the fifteen minutes he was allowed. Half the time he didn't even hear the other guys talking and joking; mostly he looked at the sky and soaked up the daylight. Then the whistle blew, and it was time to go back in and face gray walls and concrete floors.

He kept looking for other jobs, something that would get him outside. A job opened at the University of Minnesota Southern Experiment Station in Waseca, a farm where scientists tested new crop hybrids and tried to make pigs and cows meatier and bigger. The experiment station was right next to the ag school, and many of Dad's former teachers worked at the farm in the summer. He was in familiar territory, his hometown, working alongside people he knew. He was hired as a laborer, spending long days on tractors, just like his dad, like his dad before him, and his dad before him.

LIKE DAD, MOM WAS BORN IN 1944. Like the Hagers, the Zimnys were farmers and Catholic. Mom went to church at St. Mary's, a rural, whitewashed church a few miles from the farm, with its cemetery across the road. St. Mary's was nearly an exact replica of Corpus Christi, the Hagers' church.

Mom bore her father's Polish surname but inherited Irish genes from her mother, née Mary Fitzpatrick. The Irish dominated this part of the county, with Conways, Byrons, Haleys, and Mulcaheys farming the land.

Just as the churches were similar and the farming the same, the Zimnys held the same notion of "job" as the Hagers.

Grandpa Zimny farmed, just like his father before him. And Grandma Zimny was a farmwife, like her mother before her. Grandpa and Grandma Zimny raised four kids, and the path for them was the same as the Hager kids: graduate from high school, go into the service or work, get married, and have children.

Mom attended Sacred Heart High School, a square brick building on the west edge of town, next to Waseca's large brick Catholic church with its many stained-glass windows. Her brother Norbert and her sister also went to Sacred Heart, while Ray opted for Waseca's ag school, where he was a freshman when Dad was a senior. None of the Hager kids attended a Catholic school, which is surprising considering Grandma and Grandpa Hager's devout faith. I can't tell if Grandma and Grandpa Zimny were more devout or, with only four kids to raise compared to fourteen, were able to save just a bit more money. I lean toward the latter.

MOM LOVED A GOOD STORY. When she and I walked out of the Waseca public library each week, we both carried books: Stephen King, Dean Koontz, James Michener, the thick Reader's Digest Condensed Books with classic-looking covers. When she wasn't mowing or baking or making supper or cleaning, she was reading. On lazy, rainy summer afternoons or cold winter days, she sat in our upstairs living room, the tiny twelve-inch black-and-white TV tuned to CBS channel 12—the only channel it received—for background noise. Evenings, too, if she was in the midst of an especially good story. We would all be in the same room but doing our own things. She read a book, Dad worked on a puzzle or slept, and I mindlessly watched TV.

Our lives lacked drama, at least from my perspective. Quiet, midwestern. Red meat for supper every night. Vikings games on fall Sundays. Mom's books allowed her to escape: to the shores of Australia with a priestly romance in the *The Thorn Birds*, to Renaissance Italy and the tortured mind of Michelangelo in *The Agony and the Ecstasy*.

In her books, maybe Mom was looking for the drama missing in her life, which was routine, with not much to break it up: work, make supper, watch TV, repeat. Books gave her entry into other worlds, a peek into other people's lives.

But she liked the real, too. As a family, we faithfully watched the news. During supper, Dan Rather and the *CBS Evening News* beamed from the black-and-white TV. At ten o'clock each night, we watched one of the Twin Cities news broadcasts. The TV brought sordid, unimaginable, tragic stories into our home every night, and I soaked it up. So this is how the world was. Reality was to be both admired and feared, honored and dreaded.

Mom put her books down when the news began. No fictional story could compare to what was going on out there—the Iran hostage crisis, John Lennon shot, Reagan and Gorbachev and the Cold War, the deaths from AIDS. But in Waseca there was news, too, stories rippling underneath a placid surface. No fiction could compare to those, either.

I WAITED TEN YEARS before I got up the nerve to ask Mom again about her missing year. I was seventeen; we were cleaning out her father's house after he died. I convinced myself I could handle the truth. All these years my mind had gone through different scenarios. What if she had followed a rebel boyfriend out West? What if she had been pregnant and was sent away, like so many young women of the 1960s? What if I had a half-brother or half-sister out there somewhere? Dad had been dead for two years, and I didn't speak to Renee or Andy often. Maybe a new sibling was what I needed; I secretly hoped this was Mom's story.

"I was in a convent," she said matter-of-factly. Mom had not been a teen mom; she had been a nun, or, more precisely, a postulant. She stayed at a convent where a cousin of her father's had been a nun for several years. Mom tried on this new character only to find that it didn't fit. She returned home after six months. Apparently, the character of homemaker, blue-collar worker, mother, and wife was her destiny. It had been waiting for her all along.

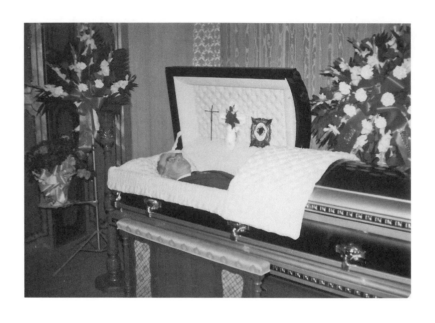

Grandpa Hager's wake, Kinder Home for Funerals, Waseca, December 1975

Chapter 4

STORMY WEATHER

$\mathcal{I}$N ONE OF MY FIRST MEMORIES, I clutch Mom's hand hard as she pulls me through the strong wind, back hunched, face shielded from the driving rain. The dangerous weather forces us from our flimsy trailer house to the safety of Grandpa Zimny's farmhouse with its stone foundation. I dared to look up, and when I did, I saw a sky painted with beautiful colors I had never seen before—pea greens swirling and mixing with soft pinks and bruised yellows. I hesitated, wanting to stare forever into the miasma, but Mom tugged on my hand and forged ahead.

The tornado stayed away that day. But in 1980, when I was five years old, a weak tornado hit our home during a freak late September storm. We were twenty miles away at a wedding dance for a cousin. Uncle Ray, who lived just a mile from us, phoned us at the dance hall. Mom and Renee and Andy and I gathered around Dad, who had ditched his suit coat and stood in his white shirt with tie loosened around his neck. "The house has been hit," Dad said as he hung up the phone. "Nothing real bad, but the trees are down." I stayed at Uncle Neil's and Aunt Donna's that night. They brought me home the next day, and I surveyed the damage in the bright, cooler sunlight. The giant elms that had lined the road were either gone or stripped of their leaves. The leaves on many of the trees never returned, permanent skeletal remains standing guard year after year. The house was perfectly intact except for shattered windows. For years afterward, I'd be on the floor playing with my Barbies only to have a shard of glass prick me on a finger and draw a droplet of blood.

In the summer, storms rolled across the prairie every few days. Just when it felt like the humidity would suffocate you, a cool front would move in and collide ferociously with the warm, moist air. Some days you could just feel a storm brewing; you could predict it as well as any psychic. The morning air would be thick and heavy, temperatures climbing well into the seventies before midmorning. I watched Grandpa's steers move more slowly than usual, and his chickens lolled around the yard as if they were in a daze.

I thrived on the excitement of an approaching summer storm, a mixture of nerves and anticipation. It was a welcome break from the quiet routine, something to provide a bit of drama. I envisioned *Wizard of Oz*–like twisters snaking out of the sky. Scary, yet awesome, a once-in-a-lifetime sight that I wanted to see badly for myself. I dared storms to come close, a challenge to God.

Some did. They advanced strong and dark blue toward our big living room window that faced west. I could see for miles across the fields; far-off lightning strikes were just short, low flashes on the horizon. I counted after each flash as I was taught in school: "One one thousand, two one thousand, three one thousand . . . " Five seconds equal one mile. I sometimes counted up to twenty before I heard a faint rumbling.

The lightning and thunder were my cue to go outside and

stand on the steps. Sometimes Mom would join me, or Dad, if he were home. I breathed in the slightly metallic scent of sulfur and something else, like rain. It's hard to describe, that smell of impending downpour, but I know the smell as well as I know the scent of a rose.

Back inside, I studied the crawl of tornado-watch counties at the bottom of the TV screen to see if Waseca County made the list. As I got older, Mom and Dad left me home alone while they mowed. If storms began to brew while I was by myself, Grandpa would telephone from next door.

"Why don't you come over?" he'd say. "The weather's gettin' pretty bad." Grandpa always insisted we come to his house during a storm. His basement walls were fashioned from thick stone and cement, a foundation that would surely withstand any storm. So I'd turn off the television and walk the well-worn path to Grandpa's.

When the tornado hit in 1980, it granted me a sense of protection. Storms would not strike the same place twice, would they? This was immunity, like the time I got chickenpox and was told I would not get it again. Worrying about a storm was one worry I could check off my list. But what else lurked out there, waiting to grab me? Heaviness always hung around me, like the air before a storm. I watched and wondered what marched invisibly toward me. I could feel it, even if I couldn't describe it.

BOOKS IN OUR HOUSE FELL APART, bits of thread hanging from spines like raw nerves. Pages from the dictionary, Dad's yearbooks, and picture books worked themselves free with the help of young fingers, first Renee's and Andy's, then mine. Grungy covers were worn at the corners. Names were printed in block letters on inside pages. An inky smile was penned on a somber Jesus in a Bible stories book. In the dictionary, the word "Monkees" was inserted next to the more traditional "monkey."

Before I could read, I sat with books open on my lap, mimicking Mom and Renee, the family bookworms. How many times did I page through these books? How many hours a day? The images remain vivid, all these years later—Curious George spilling ink all over a desk, the stripes on the hat of the cat. Most vivid, though, were the Victorian illustrations in the *Complete Mother Goose,* pictures that made my skin crawl although I didn't understand why: old men staring lecherously at young girls and effete, fat boys prancing around in bloomers or undershirts; wrinkled women with long, pointed noses, bony fingers, and bonnets on their heads.

Before there were words, there were pictures—and Mom's stories to fill them out. Mom was the midwife who delivered stories to me. She knew, or at least knew of, almost everyone in town. She knew their whispered stories. Mom possessed patience for my many questions, unlike Dad, who moved at a nervous pace thanks to caffeine and nicotine. Her stories captivated me. I'd ask her to repeat them over and over. These were daytime versions of stories told to children at the bedside. My family didn't do bedtime stories; the worlds that Mom recreated were very real.

The most tattered book in our house was the thick softcover printed to commemorate the 1967 tornado that killed six people in Waseca. Mom kept it on a high shelf, but I often asked her to fetch it for me. The pages were dog-eared and torn. On each page, black-and-white pictures detailed the twister's damage. I knew these farms, these streets. The tornado struck the southeast part of town, a neighborhood that we passed through each time we went to Woodville. Mom made the pictures come alive. The lines between past and present blurred. "The tornado came right down this street," Mom would tell me, one hand on the steering wheel, the other hand motioning to the houses as we headed to Woodville. I saw rebirth after destruction. Spindly trees with little shade had replaced the former leafy oaks and elms. Siding and roofs on the World War II–era bungalows were now bright and clean. The damage had been repaired, a wound completely healed. If Mom hadn't told me, I would have never guessed the tornado ripped apart the home of Betty, the kindly, raven-haired woman who served lunch at Hartley, while she was still in it. Or that it struck the house of Harley, the shriveled old man who was outside every day in the summer, dressed in a long-sleeved work shirt and work pants like Dad's, stooping down to pick bright blooms for his dandelion wine. We'd drive by and wave at Harley, and he'd wave in return.

MOM SAW THE STORM THAT DAY—not the actual dancing black snake of the twister, but she saw the clouds and darkness advance across the sky. In late April 1967, she was twenty-two years old and five months pregnant with Andy. I often asked her to repeat the story, trying to inhabit that place and time myself, to feel the danger and the unknown.

"It was a strange morning, warm and rainy," she'd say. "Not hot, like when you get summer storms. In fact, it was cloudy most of the day." It was a Sunday, so she and Dad and Renee, not quite two years old, went to the Hager farm on the north side of the county, as many of the Hager siblings did on Sunday afternoons.

"I could see how black it was to the south, over Waseca. When we left after supper, the highway patrol detoured us around town because Highway 14 was closed around Clear Lake," she said.

Mom's story always made me pause and think, and I asked her to tell it often. What if they had left the farm earlier that day? Might they have been swept away? Her words revealed the precariousness of a day, how you can wake up one morning and by evening an entire landscape has changed.

WE PASSED THE RUX HOUSE each time we drove Highway 14 around Clear Lake. Mom told me how the tornado's force sucked Mr. and Mrs. Rux from the house and flung their bodies into the lake. I wondered what I would have seen had I been there that day. I imagined two bodies sailing calmly, almost floating, through the air, making a gentle splash into the water. In my mind, I saw them die. At home, I stared hard at their portraits printed in the book. Here they were alive. At Woodville, Mom took me by the hand and led me to their graves on the south end. Alive, dead. Alive, dead.

IN THE BACK OF OUR RED PHOTO ALBUM were pictures of Grandpa Hager. Dead.

The four pictures were from the wake in 1975, the year I turned one. One picture shows a long-range view, as mourners would have seen Grandpa if approaching the casket straight-on, ready to sink onto the kneeler before him, head bowed, to utter an Our Father or Hail Mary. The casket centers the frame, bouquets on either side staged in perfect symmetry, the heavy draperies of Kinder's funeral home a deep gray.

Each of the next three shots provided a close, closer, and closest view of Grandpa's face. One was taken from the foot of the casket, another a step or two closer, and finally the flash on the last one washed out Grandpa's face. Grandpa wore a brown suit and green print tie, his signature horn-rimmed glasses balanced on the bridge of his nose. Propped in the coffin's lid was a Knights of Columbus plaque, a spray of eight roses from his great-grandchildren, and a crucifix.

A DAY OR TWO before the heart attack killed him instantly at age seventy-one, a week before Christmas, Grandpa called each of his six daughters. This was unusual in two ways. For one, he wasn't much of a talker, his laconic manner offsetting Grandma's constant yapping. And two, he was tight with money, too tight to make long-distance phone calls. He was a product of the Depression, memories still fresh of dusty days farming the land and saving each penny to put food on the table. But on that day, he carefully dialed Loretta and Helen and Rosanne and Susie and Sandy and Debbie.

You'll all be here on Christmas Day, right? he asked each daughter. *Your Ma will be home from the hospital, and I wanna make sure that you'll all be here. It'll make her so happy.*

An arthritic back had landed Grandma in the hospital, decades of farm labor and birthing sixteen children catching up to her. She was still in the hospital when her Hank died. It was just him and Uncle Davey on the farm that day. Grandpa was walking from the house to the barn when his heart stopped. He collapsed in a heap outside the front door. It would be the way of death for so many Hager men.

Dad called Mom at work: "Dad's dead," he said. He asked her to tell two relatives who worked at the factory with her: Neil's wife, Donna, and Aunt Marie, Hank's sister. Mom found Donna, and together they walked to Marie's cubicle. Marie crumpled like a piece of paper; tears streamed down her face. Mom and Donna ushered her to the nurse's station, and they held her hand while she wept for her brother.

The Hager kids debated how to tell Grandma that her husband had died. Who would tell her? Should they all go into the hospital room? Or just one? Which one? Loretta, the oldest? John, the oldest boy? Who? In the end, they washed their hands of the task and handed the responsibility to the parish priest.

The doctor granted Grandma a release from the hospital to briefly attend the wake. Her kids wheeled her into the funeral home, just long enough to gaze at Grandpa's face one last time, then back to the hospital. That's why Uncle Gene took the casket pictures, so Grandma would have something to hold, a way to remember. Copies were made for each of the kids.

I can't pinpoint the exact moment I first saw those pictures. There must have been a day when I said *Who is this?* and Mom and Dad responded, *That's your Grandpa Hager, your dad's dad.* Perhaps if the photos had shocked me, or if I had stumbled on them in a secret moment, the memory would be crisp. But instead the pictures were ordinary. Just another snapshot of our family, another piece of history, another picture of the dead.

Grandpa didn't look much different in his casket than he did in the few family photos we had of him. The heart attack left his body unbruised, unbroken. In the pictures of him living, in posed studio shots of the Hager family, Grandpa towered above his wife and fourteen surviving kids at six-foot-two. He was usually unsmiling and appeared uncomfortable, as if his bones were too big for his skin, his face dogged and weary as if he had just come in from the fields. He was the only one who didn't smile in pictures, stoicism next to Grandma's cheery mug and the cherubic grins of the kids.

Next to the visitation photos were two pictures of Grandpa's casket from the cemetery the day of his funeral. He was buried at Corpus Christi, a small cemetery across the road in the shadow of a white-washed church. I liked whispering "Corpus Christi, Corpus Christi"; the name flowed off my tongue. Even the name invoked death, a Latin "body of Christ" transported to southern Minnesota. The cemetery had a life-sized marble statue of Jesus dead on the cross, Mary and John the Baptist kneeling at his feet.

CORPUS CHRISTI had been the Hagers' church since they moved a couple of miles down the road thirty years before. It was a mild November day in 1943 when Grandpa journeyed to the last place he'd call home. The era was in transition—everyone had cars, but horses and wagons still were an integral part of the farm. Instead of renting a trailer, Grandpa elected to drive his team of four horses fifteen miles from the Waterville farm to the new farm in Blooming Grove Township. My older aunts and uncles say he left that morning—turning around to wave at his wife and kids—on a wagon filled with hay, posts, oats, a hay loader, and two five-gallon pails of water for the horses. The landscape rolled with hills; he stopped halfway up steep inclines, placed posts behind the wagon wheels to keep them from slipping backward, and gave the horses a rest. The trip took seven hours. The rest of the family followed the next day, a Friday, and any relative who could spare a car or truck packed it with clothes, dishes, beds, chairs, and a table. The cattle arrived in two large trucks. Grandpa and Grandma had planned to sweep through the doors of their new church that Sunday with their nine kids in tow and Grandma's belly just starting to bulge with Dad, but a snowstorm cancelled their plans. Dad was the first Hager to be baptized at Corpus Christi, water splashing cold over his smooth forehead. The church was where the siblings squirmed in hard wooden pews, quietly whispering, joking, poking each other, but always under the watchful eyes of their dad, who tried to stop their antics with one harsh glance. If that didn't work, then a trip down the aisle, strong arm firmly grasping small arm, to outside the church doors where he delivered a hard swat on the butt.

THE DAY OF GRANDPA'S FUNERAL was one of those quiet winter days, a day in which the sky and clouds wove a thick blanket that chokes out sound. In a Minnesota winter, at a rural cemetery eight miles from the nearest tiny town, deafening silence is not cliché. In one picture from the graveside, three dark-clad men walk toward the church, seen on the far right side of the frame, the sound of their shoes crunching on snow seeming to lift from the photo. Far away and barely visible, the casket sits suspended above the grave, awaiting placement in the vault and then the cold December ground.

A second picture shows Corpus Christi in the background, straight-on center, its simple white steeple rising high above the leafless hardwoods that appear all but dead and the evergreens that hold their dark color despite the chill. This picture reveals a closer view of the casket; it rests on top of the wide straps that balance it over the vault already in the grave. The dirt at the grave's side is covered with a fuzzy green tarp. I knew this prop well from Dad's job; he used it to cover the grim reality of grave dirt. Grandpa's grave was at the cemetery's edge, near trees and wild prairie, a field lightly dusted with snow in the distance.

Near these pictures in the photo album was another picture,

a Polaroid. In it, Dad sits cross-legged on the floor in front of the Christmas tree with dots of red, green, and yellow lights. Renee sits to his left. Andy kneels on Dad's right, his arm extended across Dad's shoulders. I am a baby on Dad's lap, with short, frizzy hair—only my dress defines me as a girl. I wear no expression, instead looking blankly ahead. But everyone else is grinning widely with holiday cheer. The date at the bottom is December 22, 1975, the day of Grandpa Hager's funeral.

The pictures of Grandpa Hager were developed, and Grandma received her copies, as did all the kids. Mom placed the pictures in an album with a red cover, the word "photos" italicized and embossed in gold on the front. She put them toward the back, past pictures of Renee holding a northern pike, Andy posing with kittens in front of the red barn, and me, a naked baby on the rug. She arranged the casket photos on the sticky page and smoothed the shiny plastic protector over them. She pressed down gently, sealing them forever into the album, and brought them into the family fold.

AT GRANDPA ZIMNY'S HOUSE, there were no pictures of anyone, dead or alive. No photo albums, no picture frames on the walls. No pictures of Grandma Zimny. I was four when she died, but small scenes of her remain in my mind. I spent full days at Grandma and Grandpa's house; they lived next door in an old farmhouse, and Grandma watched me while Mom and Dad worked their day jobs, before they had the cemetery business. Grandma mostly sat either at the kitchen table or on the couch, reading the newspaper, pulling a tissue from her bra to wipe her nose. We'd watch Julia Child on television, and I wondered why she chose to cook with those gargantuan rings on her fingers.

Shortly after Grandma died, I was exploring all parts of the house—bedroom drawers, the attic, the musty basement. Next to Grandpa's brown leather recliner in the living room was a small table with a lamp on top and a box of tissues. The table had two drawers, which I pulled open while Grandpa watched television. Inside, I saw several loose Polaroids with Grandma as the subject. I reached down and started to grab the pictures when Grandpa stopped me.

"Don't go in there," he said quietly. He got up from his chair and shut the drawers.

GRANDPA HAGER'S POSTMORTEM PICTURES were a microcosm of how death infiltrated our lives, how we let it in without question. Once, a funeral director in California sent Dad the ashes of a man to be buried in Waseca. The plain white box, wrapped over and over with clear packaging tape, sat on our clothes dryer for a week or so, waiting for graveside services to be arranged. That man—I never knew his name—was part of our family for a while, bouncing and vibrating every time Mom did a load of laundry.

For me, Grandpa's casket pictures were puzzle pieces that made up his life story, and pictures of him at his First Communion, at his wedding, and with his children revealed his narrative. We welcomed Grandpa's spirit, invited it to commune with us among the other pictures of our living family.

How do we learn to make meaning? We aren't delivered into this world with a breadth of knowledge. Pictures were my first introduction to a world that could be brutal and unpredictable. Pictures introduced me to the fact that though people may be gone from this earth, something of them lives on. The pictures represented their souls, which surely still existed.

* * *

AT WOODVILLE, I come across a reddish-brown granite grave-stone. Something shiny at the top catches my eye—a bronzed clasp with a faux-aged finish, a larger version of a locket a mother might wear around her neck. The clasp is irresistible to my young fingers. I kneel onto the earth before Vicki. I reach out to touch the metal warmed by the sun, and lift the lid.

Vicki Mittelsteadt, in the genesis of adolescence, beams at me. Her smile glows, teeth even and white, cheeks flushed pink. A kelly green jacket complements her red hair, the patterned collar of a shirt layered underneath, fashionably 1970s.

Her picture looks so alive that I cannot imagine someone like her being dead. She should have been in English class, hatching weekend plans with her girlfriends. She should have been calling boys on the phone, quickly hanging up when they answered, her heart pounding. She should have been lying in her bed at night, the warm summer breeze tickling the curtains, dreaming of her future, imagining far-off places that she would visit, cities where she would live. She should not have been at Woodville. Not yet.

I became obsessed with Vicki. Each time I'm at Woodville, a couple of days a week, I commune with her at her grave. As the years go by, I wonder about different things. I wonder how she died. I wonder if she knew she was dying. I try to imagine that feeling, and I shudder.

I wonder about Vicki's mom. How might it feel to watch a child die? My friend Heidi's mom, Marian, watched her son die with a disease so rare doctors considered naming it after him. I saw the way Marian's face pinched. Even when her mouth smiled, her eyes did not. If I had ever seen her without a shirt,

I knew I'd be able to count her ribs. Heidi's dad was big, as rotund as ever. Maybe grief just wasted moms.

So I always think about Vicki's mom, never her dad. What if someone could have warned her when she was young, just married, that she would bury a daughter? What if she got a visit from her future self? Would she have fled from the altar, away from the young groom standing there, veil flying, heels clacking down cement church steps?

I imagine the day her mom picked out the gravestone and decided to include the picture. A larger version of Vicki's portrait probably stood on the television set at home or hung on a wall going up the stairs, next to the pictures of her older brothers and sisters. Her mom also thinks about the inscriptions, what the marker should look like, what it should say. At the top, simply engraved, is "Daughter." At the bottom, a line from Psalm 23, "The Lord is my Shepherd." A shining star—the star of Bethlehem, the star that marked a child's birth—is carved between Vicki's birth date (April 1, 1961) and the date of her death (September 29, 1976). She is beautiful, yet dead. But the beauty of her, the beauty around me, rarely allows reality to sink in.

I WAS A ROMANTIC MISPLACED IN A MODERN AGE. In the late eighteenth century, the Romantics liberated themselves from logic and sought to distance themselves from the cold calculations wrung from the age of reason. They traveled to realms of emotion and imagination and created alternate worlds in which to escape. The Romantic poet William Wordsworth suggested that we could do more than passively perceive the world around us: we also could actively create for ourselves a world in which we wanted to live. The Romantics used imagination to bring together disparate ideas, to synthesize opposite and contradictory messages.

The Romantics were obsessed with the exotic and things and ideas that run contrary to reason, the juxtaposition of the natural and supernatural—life and death, beauty and ugliness, novelty and familiarity. The literary epitome of this obsession with paradox takes form in *The Hunchback of Notre Dame* and *Frankenstein*, books that feature characters ugly on the outside but beautiful on the inside. In music, Beethoven and Schubert created compositions of intense expressiveness, displaying a willingness to forsake traditional classical forms. Goya and Delacroix painted passionate violence wrapped in the arms of sublime beauty.

This was an era of elaborate funerals and extravagant mourning clothes. The dead were laid out in plush caskets and surrounded with heavenly bouquets and pictures, always pictures. Postmortem photographs were taken in which living relatives posed with the dead for a final family portrait. And pictures, much like Vicki's, were made small for lockets or brooches. The ugliness of death was given a beautiful veneer.

And what did I see every day? Not the harsh reality. Naked, dead flesh was handled well away from the public; fluids and stink were kept in basement prep rooms at Kinder's and Sandberg's. I was left with the beauty. By the time the dead arrived at the cemetery, the caskets—rich wood, elaborately carved, accented with brass handles—were closed, with redolent sprays of roses and carnations on top. In the quiet of Dad's cemeteries, the dead were tucked neatly into the ground, unseen but still there.

Dad and Mom didn't notice how I lingered at Vicki's grave. No one asked how the picture of a dead teenager might affect me. The thoughts I had about mortality and dying were mine alone. Dad and Mom operated under the expectation that if death was routine to them, it would be routine for me and Renee and Andy, too. Death was an integral part of Dad and Mom's landscape—gravestones, caskets, and funerals were so familiar they didn't even see them anymore, just as commuters don't see the landmarks they drive past each day. Dad and Mom assumed that because their kids lived in the world of the dead, we would automatically know it. We would intuit death and somehow absorb its complexities through osmosis. Words describing death never escaped our lips. Perhaps speaking of it would make it too real.

I PLUNGED MYSELF INTO A WORLD OF FAIRY TALES, continuing to create my own version of the world, a world of happy endings and everlasting life, where the young and beautiful stayed that way forever. I drank in the stories of Cinderella, Rumpelstiltskin, Rapunzel, Sleeping Beauty. I paged through the richly illustrated books with pictures of turreted castles, gold-filled rooms, and lush forests. These stories recorded by the Brothers Grimm have their roots in Germany, as did I. At the height of the Romantic era, the brothers traveled throughout the separate nation-states that would later become Germany, writing down ancient folktales told by wizened men and fleshy women. The Grimms saw themselves as the keepers of the stories.

Their stories often featured a heroine in a white dress. "Happily ever after" implied a wedding, which was the ultimate goal of any girl, including me. Marriage was the antideath. My cousin Bernadette and I were obsessed with weddings and with wedding dresses in particular. Each time a Hager cousin got married (which happened two or three times a year), Bernadette and I swooned over the dress. At the reception hall, we sidled up to the bride, touched the white silk or satin fabric with our fingers, and whispered breathlessly, "It's so beautiful."

Bernadette was the girl cousin on Dad's side closest to my age, just ten months older. Each summer she spent a week at my house, and I spent a week at hers. One of the first things we'd do when we were together was to throw a bridal magazine or two in the grocery cart when we went shopping with our moms. At home, we sat close together with the magazine on our laps, our fingers turning the slick, perfumed pages. We oohed and ahhed over the different dresses, lush, white gowns with long trains, lace, and ruffles. In the visions of our weddings, we didn't need a groom. We saw only ourselves walking down the aisle, our mere beauty causing the eyes of guests to mist. We saw an altar with only bridesmaids lined up on one side, no groomsmen on the other. We pictured the bridesmaids in fuschia, emerald green, even black. We named our bridesmaids: I would have Renee, my cousin Karen, and Bernadette; she would have her sister Jolene, and me for sure.

We sashayed down imaginary aisles, practicing the slow, careful steps of a bride. Our moms supplied the dresses. At Bernadette's, I encased her in her mother's dress. Dozens of tiny buttons marched up the back. It took me forever to slip them through their fabric loops. My fingers were thin and long, like Mom's, but still I fumbled. At my house, Bernadette zipped me up in Mom's dress. Our moms' dresses were small—they fit amazingly well over our pre-pubescent hips and breasts. My mom's dress was disappointingly boring—no lace, no buttons. Quiet, like her. I coveted Bernadette's pretty, cherished heirloom and wanted one for myself. I had seen wedding pictures of Grandma and Grandpa Hager and wondered if Grandma still had the knee-length shift dress so perfectly symbolic of the

Roaring Twenties. I dreamed of wearing an heirloom, a way to keep alive a piece of the past.

A SENSE OF UNFAIRNESS draws me to Vicki's grave again and again. For years, every time I walked by Vicki's stone, I opened and closed, opened and closed that clasp, fascinated by the photograph underneath, hoping the next time I opened it she wouldn't be there, that she wouldn't really be dead.

But she was always there. She was a reminder that anyone could die at any time. Cemeteries were filled with examples, and I walked among them every day. Why should my family be any different? Our familiarity with death could not provide a cloak to keep us safe.

Fears and worries lurked in my mind, not all-consuming, but like a low-grade fever that was always there. I wondered if I would die young, like Vicki. I wondered if disease would claim me. I watched an *ABC Afterschool Special* on a young girl with leukemia, a girl my age. When I saw strands of hair on my brush, I was convinced I had cancer. I watched TV movies about the Atlanta child murders and the kidnapping of Adam Walsh. Would I, too, fall victim to the same fate? Every time I turned on the television, it seemed there was something else that could kill me. In 1981, I watched a *60 Minutes* report on a new disease assailing our cities. Mostly young men and prostitutes were coming down with illnesses that would not go away, illnesses that morphed into pneumonia or cancer that eventually killed them. Something, a type of virus, seemed to be shutting down their immune systems. Was this new disease, this disease they called AIDS, something for me to fear?

I wondered if an accident would claim my parents. For a time, I habitually asked Mom every day when I left for school:

"Will you be home when I get home?" I waited for the day that she wouldn't be there when I got off the school bus, when she wouldn't be getting supper ready. I could see the day when Dad wouldn't be there, stoking the fire in our wood-burning stove or putting together a jigsaw puzzle. I demanded that they reassure me. Because if they said they would be there, that meant it was true, so I could rest easy for another day.

I LINGERED at the pictures of Vicki, Grandpa, the Ruxes. I was trying to find the story, a story that would help me make sense of the world. Stories weren't just make-believe, all Dr. Seuss and Mother Goose. I saw a circle: first life, then death. Spring, summer, fall, winter. Blue sky and storms and quilts of cold clouds occupy the same space but at different times. Memories and stories help you rebuild. Things most precious to you may be gone, lost to the wicked wind, but you remember what had been, and you move on.

The Zimmerman gravestone, Calvary Cemetery, Waseca

Chapter 5

PRECIOUS IN THE SIGHT
OF THE LORD IS THE
DEATH OF HIS SAINTS

*I*N 1980, DAD DUG UNCLE HAROLD'S GRAVE. Harold was only fifty years old, but years of hard drinking had taken their toll. The Hagers liked their booze, and Uncle Harold, who married into the family, fit in well.

We got together often for holidays and weddings and graduations. These gatherings flowed with the Hager version of milk and honey—beer and whiskey—and the slurred words that went along. Drunken uncles, about a dozen at any given time, huddled over card tables, playing euchre and pfeffer in foursomes. Smoke wafted over their heads like mist. Cigarettes were balanced between their lips and left their mouths only long enough for swigs of liquor. Coins and bills spread across tables, changing hands as quickly as glasses and bottles emptied. Staccato outbursts of *God dammit!* or *Jesus Christ!* punctuated raucous laughter. My uncles (and an occasional aunt, like the tough-talking Aunt Harriet) rarely uttered *fuck* or *shit*. In that Catholic family, taking the Lord's name in vain was the ultimate curse.

Every so often, one of the uncles would rise unsteadily from his rickety chair. He'd walk past my cousins and me and say

Havin' fun? or *Goddamn your dad, he's takin' all my money,* exhaling pungent breath in our faces. Bernadette and Julie and Carrie and I giggled as he swayed back to the games. We had no way of knowing that not every family drank this much.

Memories of Uncle Harold fuzz around the edges. I mostly know him through a few family pictures and 8 mm films, where he's robust and pink-cheeked. But I remember him best for his death. I was five years old. Harold was a big guy with a boisterous guffaw, bowling ball paunch, and few hairs on his head. His last Christmas, he sat quietly in a corner of Grandma's kitchen, his body withered, skin wrinkled. Could he have really been only fifty? He looked so old, like a grandpa, not an uncle.

On the day of Harold's funeral, the family gathered around the ground's open wound in Woodville's new addition, wide open and grassy with plenty of room for expansion. Only two rows of stones ran the length of the section, with Harold's grave in front along the road. The priest talked and we stood silent, eyes lowered in reverence.

Except for me. I focused on Michelle, Harold's only daughter, the prize at the tail end of four boys. Tall and sturdy like her brothers, she had graduated from high school not long before. She was the only one openly crying. Everyone else stood stoic and strong, a finger here and there reaching to wipe a tear. But Michelle wasn't just crying; she was sobbing. Her long blond hair covered the face she buried in her mother's shoulder, and her back heaved.

Michelle's emotion frightened me, but I couldn't look away. I felt as embarrassed for her as I would have felt had she been physically naked. I shifted my weight and squirmed. I wanted someone to smooth everything over, to make her stop. Couldn't she tell that I was staring at her, that others were staring? She was not in control, and this was a place where control was prized. You worked long days to get ahead; you carefully managed every action to give off an air of success. To show chinks in that armor—to fail at work, to fail at emotional control— was unthinkable.

Even at five years old, I sensed that Michelle's display should be private and that I was an intruder. She should be at home in her room crying, not here. Why I thought that, I do not know. It wasn't intuition. Intuition would tell me it's a natural human response to cry and wail and grieve with others. But over time, that's been pushed down, at least in our culture. I caught on to that early. The body in the casket is perfumed and made up. Green artificial turf is used to cover the mound of dirt at the gravesite. The funeral director carefully guides and choreographs every move to be sure nothing falls out of line. We had ways to neatly bottle up death, so we did. This is what I absorbed from my earliest days.

The day of Uncle Harold's funeral, something quickened inside of me. I didn't have a name for it. All I knew is that I wanted to run to Michelle and ask her to stop crying. Maybe she would stop if I gave her a hug, comforted her somehow. But I stayed safely next to Mom, tightly gripping her hand. Yet for the first time I understood that when Dad buried a body, a family cried. This was Michelle's dad, someone she loved and cared for, going into the ground. This wasn't just another body, another anonymous procession. These mourners were family.

The cemetery took on a different meaning. It became more than an expanse of lawn marked with jutting granite and marble teeth, more than just a place where Dad and Mom worked. It was no longer the place where I sat in the pickup with my books until I could go home and play with my Barbies. Instead, the places where I watered flowers or picked up sticks were the same places families like Michelle's had stood. Holes were opened to receive their bounty, then closed forever. Bodies rested below me, invisible tenants. As this realization grew and became stronger, I wondered about the dead in our cemeteries and the people they had left behind.

WHEN UNCLE HAROLD DIED, the gravestones had just started speaking to me in faint whispers. The stories were quiet at first, a dull hum that resonated from the ground. But now they grew louder, more insistent. I read names, calculated ages, but still, that didn't tell me everything. Some gravestones revealed tantalizing clues—a young death, a picture of the dead, or multiple deaths in the same family in the same year. But I couldn't discern how they had died. For that I needed help, a translator—Mom.

When Mom finished mowing, she sometimes helped me rake grass from the gravestones. Mostly we were quiet, the tines of our rakes scraping granite like long fingernails. But at times I paused, read a name, calculated an age, and asked *What happened?* Mom always had answers and was willing to share.

One monument and its story stood apart from the thousands of others in our cemeteries. At Calvary, Waseca's Catholic cemetery, two intersecting gravel roads divided the cemetery into four sections, and a road circled the perimeter. I rode endless loops on my bike. On the cemetery's back road, near the woods, I always slowed my bike and turned my head toward one particular monument, as if I were gawking at a wreck on the highway. I could never look away from the Zimmerman gravestone. The height of the gray granite slab wasn't unusual—just a couple of feet off the ground. But its length was impossible to miss:

twenty-four feet. The length of four men the size of Dad, lying head to toe.

Here, Jim Zimmerman's first wife lies buried, along with a daughter, a daughter, a son, a daughter, a daughter, a son, and a daughter. The year of death for all of them, 1959, repeats again and again, a skipping record. A stillborn baby girl, 1959–1959. Jan, 1957–1959. James, 1953–1959. Barbara, 1951–1959. Constance, 1950–1959. Michael, 1949–1959. Kathryn, 1947–1959. And the mother, Irene, 1926–1959.

I asked Mom about the Zimmermans.

ON SEPTEMBER 11, 1959, Irene loaded her six kids into the family's boat of a station wagon to cart them to Sacred Heart Catholic School. Jan wasn't in school yet, but she clambered into the car with her brothers and sisters. Irene turned right onto Highway 14 for the two-mile trek into town, as Jim continued the morning's farm work.

Irene drove along the highway, past Clear Lake on her right and the Victorian and Queen Anne houses built on nineteenth-century wheat money on her left. She crossed Main Street. A couple of blocks ahead were the railroad tracks and just past the tracks, one more block, stood Sacred Heart.

It's impossible to know exactly what Irene saw or what she was thinking as she approached the tracks. Maybe she saw the train coming from her left, but misjudged its speed. Maybe the kids were squirming and hitting each other, and she turned back to scold them. Maybe they were all singing a song, and Irene missed the whistle.

At 8:05 a.m., Irene collided with a Minneapolis & St. Louis train heading south to Peoria, Illinois. The train, with sixty-four cars, was running late; it had been scheduled to rumble through town at 6:30. Witnesses said the train was traveling at least forty-five miles per hour when Irene inched across the tracks.

Car passengers in train-car collisions almost never survive; the inequality of mass and momentum is too great. The train weighed eight thousand tons. The 1959 Dodge station wagon weighed one and three-quarter tons at most. A train hitting a car is like a car hitting a soda can. The engineer could do nothing but pull the emergency switch and hope for the best. The train traveled another one-third of a mile before finally stopping.

Irene and Kathryn lived for a few minutes after the collision; the others died instantly. The priest from Sacred Heart heard the ferocious noise and came running; he administered Last Rites. Blood was rushed from a nearby hospital, state patrol officers escorting the ambulance, but it was too late to save anyone.

I listened to Mom tell the story and asked to hear it again and again. Tragedies of this magnitude happened only on television. I couldn't believe this had occurred in my town, to people Mom knew. She dropped in new information from time to time: how the Zimmermans' wake was held at their home because no funeral parlor could hold seven caskets; how Mom's sister, Margaret, went to the visitation because it was traditional for seniors at Sacred Heart to go to parish wakes.

SHADOWS OF JIM AND MICHELLE REMAIN. They—and all others who have walked in the cemetery—leave behind a fine layer of grief on every surface, dust that's never swept away. The sadness of the bereaved is too big for one person to bear. Those of us there every day breathed it in, however invisible, and it became part of us. Yet when the grief was visible, I pushed it away. In my mind, I watched Michelle from a distance, from a spot under a tree in the next section over. Perhaps I am remembering this correctly. Mom may have stood there with me in case I talked loudly, which I was prone to do. But I think, too, that my mind created that space, opened up a distance. If I had let myself get any closer, Michelle's grief might have swallowed me, too.

At Calvary, each time I rode my bicycle on the gravel roads, I would stop at the Zimmerman monument, lay my bike on the grass, and walk a slow path around the grave. I listened. But I couldn't grasp what had happened, couldn't begin to understand how Jim went on with life after his whole family had died. It hurt my mind, like when I thought about the infinity of the universe. I had to turn away. Jim's energy was still there in that place, pieces of his hurt and grief and sadness. I felt it, if only for an impossibly brief moment. Then I pedaled away, powered by the surge. But always, at Calvary, I would come back, unable to stay away from the story etched in stone. The words on the front speak of Irene and the children. But the back of the monument speaks of Jim. I knew his thoughts without even knowing him, just by reading what was etched there: *Precious in the sight of the Lord is the death of his saints.*

Great-grandparents Mary and Vincent Zimny *(seated)*, with witnesses
Elizabeth Yokiel and Ignatius (Andrew) Zimny

Chapter 6

BREAK THE PLOW

*F*ROM THE KITCHEN WINDOW of the house where I lived as a child, I looked out on Grandpa's farmhouse. I spied on Grandpa as he walked down his front steps, stooped to feed his mutt, Barney, and ambled toward his weathered barn. Beneath his trademark Oshkosh pinstripe overalls and chambray shirt, Grandpa's upper back rounded, and he pitched forward from his hips when he walked. His leg joints moved in a rhythm different from the rest of him, as if controlled by an amateur puppeteer who didn't know when to pull the strings. One day, I asked Mom why.

She filled her mixer with flour and sugar and added eggs she had grabbed from the barn that morning, making yet another batch of cookies. "Grandpa's parents died of the flu when he was just six or seven," she said, pressing the lever on the mixer so it stirred. "His uncle Paul took him in because he was his godfather. Paul put him to work right away. One of his first jobs was lifting rocks out of those North Dakota fields. His back never recovered."

A child, my age, bending to take a rock from its bed. Too heavy, yet he lifts, curling his body around the bulk, cradling it in his arms. Walks unsteadily to the wagon hitched to the horse team. Lets the rock fall with a thud into the wagon. Straightens out the best he can and heads back to the field, over and over.

WE DON'T SEE THE SOIL turn beneath our feet. It isn't like a swift-moving river; it turns at its own steady pace. Buried within the soil are heavy stones, debris left behind when long-ago glaciers retreated north. Each spring, some of those stones make it to the surface, pushed up by the thawing movement of the dirt. And worms—tens of thousands wiggling and roiling in just one acre—spawn enough movement to constantly shift the soil. Fieldstones poke their heads out of the ground. If left there, they will damage a plow's blade, and so they must be removed. In Grandpa's youth, farmers were just breaking the virgin North Dakota prairie, priming the ancient land covered in prairie grass for its new role supporting wheat and corn. Rocks were everywhere.

Today, these fieldstones decorate lawns throughout the Midwest. If you want rocks, just ask a farmer, and he'll point to where he keeps his pile of fieldstones. "Sure, take as many as you want," he'll say, and off you go with free lawn adornments. Dad uncovered a large boulder once in one of his graves. The vault guy used the cranks and pulleys that usually lowered bodies into the ground to lift out the rock and place it in the back of Dad's truck. Dad gifted the rock to Mom, a rock from a grave that served as a lovely centerpiece in her flower bed.

Why do we speak of the earth as terra firma? Why, after a harrowing plane ride, do we kiss the ground? We think of it as solid, but the earth's surface façade masks the turmoil under us. Soil expands and contracts, freezes, thaws, cracks, rises, sinks, and worms move through the dirt, paving the way for water and air to flow through and shift the soil. It happens so slowly that we cannot feel it. We don't notice the change until a giant rock emerges and breaks the plow.

IN A SMALL FARMHOUSE near Lansford, North Dakota, in 1918, my mother's father sleeps soundly in a big bed with his three brothers. Moans penetrate the quiet of seven-year-old Gregory's sleep, and he stirs. The sounds poke at his dreams, a pin that prods, pushes, then finally breaks through. He opens his eyes, sticky with sleep. For a moment he doesn't know where he is, the transition from dream to reality too abrupt. He rolls over, stretches his arms, and rubs his eyes. The day's first light— a cold blue that only December can bring—streams into the bedroom. Gregory doesn't know what day it is. He's been sleeping, on and off, for days, never leaving the bed. He remembers hazy scenes: waking up in the night, cold sweat crawling over his skin; waking during the day, too hot, throwing off his bed covers, clawing at his nightgown; people at his bedside, a cavalcade of women—tall women, thin women, stout women. He recognized only one, his aunt Agnes from the next farm. The women placed cool washcloths on his forehead and spoke to him in quiet, gentle murmurs, combinations of Polish and English. The smoothness of the voices lulled him back to sleep. A thought enters his mind: where was his mom? He doesn't remember her at his bedside.

The thought leaves as he takes inventory of his body. Today feels different. The aches that were married to Gregory's bones are now gone. The fog that throbbed in his head has left, too. The last time he was awake, it was light. Now it's light again. He figures he must have been asleep for a very long time. He probably would have slept longer, too, if it weren't for the moans.

Instinct tells him they come from his mom. He recognizes the timbre of her voice, even though he's not heard these animal sounds before. When did he last see her? He thinks back, hard. It was the first day he felt ill, days ago. She had helped Gregory into his nightclothes and ushered him to bed with his brothers and one sister. She reached down and placed the back of her hand on his forehead. A brief, dark shadow crossed her face; her smile faded when she touched the dry hotness of his skin. She kissed his cheek, leaned over, and planted kisses on his brothers. She straightened, placed her hand on her taut belly, and stiffly walked out of the room. He didn't know it then, but it's that image that will always come back to him before sleep on so many nights all his years. When he's an old man, when a massive heart attack kills him on his front lawn, he will see his young mother walking away, and then he will follow.

The moans this morning are the result of the baby in Mary's belly making its way out. Gregory rolls to his side and swings his legs to the floor. He stands, unsteady, like the newborn calves in the barn. Blood rushes to his head and he wobbles, nearly falling over in a dizzy rush. He hasn't stood for days. He grabs on to the wooden headboard and takes a couple of breaths. His lungs feel tight, but he no longer coughs. In the bed, Ed and Fabian and Norbert rest, their cheeks flushed. Gregory walks out of the room, the sounds a luring siren song.

He stops in the doorway of his parents' bedroom. Mary lies on the bed, her waxy face slick with sweat. In between cries, she collapses back to her pillow and breathes heavily. The rasps sound like branches scraping a window. She coughs hard. Two women hold up her head. Gregory sees his older sister, Alice, bring a rag to Mary's mouth. When Alice tosses the rag to the floor, Gregory sees it's covered with blood. He gasps. Alice spins around and spies him. She places her hands on his bony shoulders and ushers him from the room.

Gregory twists and turns to look at his mom, but Alice is stronger and bigger and he's forced out of the doorway; the door shuts on him. He stands for a moment, looking at the barrier before him. He turns around and sees his dad on a makeshift cot by the fireplace. Gregory tiptoes toward Vincent. Vincent's lips are parched, and his breath wheezes and crackles in tandem with the fireplace. His eyes flutter open. He gasps and writhes. He moves his lips, but no words come out. Gregory looks around and spots a tin cup nearby, full of water. He brings it to his father's lips.

Vincent drinks, then coughs hard. White mucus, tinged with blood, comes out of his mouth. He speaks, barely audible. Gregory recognizes the words as Polish: "Święta Maryjo, Matko Boża, módl się za nami grzesznymi teraz i w godzinę śmierci naszej." *(Holy Mary, mother of God, pray for us sinners now and at the hour of our death.)*

There are shrieks from the bedroom. Gregory straightens and rushes into the room. This time, he's too fast for Alice. He darts away from her reach and runs to the wooden dresser. There, on top in a ceramic box, lies Vincent's rosary. Gregory grabs it and looks up. His eyes meet Alice's. She relaxes and nods when she sees what Gregory clutches in his hands.

Gregory jogs back to his dad and interlaces the beads between Vincent's thick, dirt-stained fingers. He weakly clasps his rosary. Slowly, he mutters the prayers. The beads advance slowly, almost imperceptibly. Gregory kneels at the cot, crosses himself, and prays along. "Zdrowaś Maryjo, laski pełna Pan z Tobą, błogosławionaś Ty między niewiastami błogosławiony owoc żywota Twojego, Jezus." *(Hail Mary, full of grace, the*

Lord is with thee; blessed art thou amongst women, and blessed is the fruit of thy womb, Jesus.)

Gregory climbs onto the cot and spoons next to Vincent, one small arm flung over his dad's chest. He holds on tight and falls asleep.

He wakes a few hours later to the sounds of weak, pitiful, squawking cries. Gregory rises up and looks at his dad. Vincent's chest moves up and down, quickly and shallowly. Gregory climbs down and enters his mom's bedroom.

Two women hold a baby. He's barely moving. They lean in close to him; Alice stands nearby. One of the women baptizes the baby. There is no time to wait for the priest. He is at other houses; other people are sick with influenza, too. The baby dies within hours. The next morning, a Tuesday, Vincent dies. Mary passes that night. The three bodies are stored in the vault at the Catholic cemetery. When the ground thaws in the spring, they are buried, Mary cradling the baby in her arms.

WE GO TO CHURCH EVERY SUNDAY. We go no matter the weather, no matter the season. Even on those splendid spring and fall Sundays, when farmers like Uncle Ray and John Krause and Jerry Stencel itch to get into the fields to plant or harvest because they know it's only a matter of time before the weather changes, we go to church. On those days the priest keeps the sermon short and races through communion, and we are out the door in twenty minutes—after all, this is a rural church. But still we go.

We go even when we feel sick or tired. Only the very worst of illnesses, involving vomiting or muscle aches so severe getting out of bed is impossible, are reason enough to stay home. Staying home on Sunday mornings isn't a treat anyway, because the good television shows like *Grizzly Adams* or WWF wrestling with Mean Gene or *Mutual of Omaha's Wild Kingdom* don't come on until after we get home from church.

At precisely 9:15 each Sunday morning, Grandpa waits at the end of our sidewalk in his 1964 powder-blue Buick. I bound ahead to the car, and Mom walks with purpose while Dad lags behind. In the car, Mom, St. Joe's organist, sits in the front seat next to her father, her hands resting placidly on her music folder and large hymnbook on her lap. Dad and I plop down on the backseat.

Grandpa drives forty miles per hour all the way to church, an interminable distance of only twelve miles. I sigh loudly in frustration as Grandpa cranes his neck like so many other farmers, checking out the fields of the Donelons or the Brittons to see how his crop compares and taking mental notes for discussion after Mass on the church's front steps. My sighs always prompt a sharp backward glare from Mom. I think Dad is equally impatient, but he knows enough to be quiet.

EACH LENTEN SEASON, on frozen February and March nights, we replay the last hours of Christ's death through the Stations of the Cross. Father Gavin, wearing purple vestments the color of angry bruises, marches slowly up and down the aisle, slinging an incense burner from side to side. The thick, acrid smoke burns my nostrils and nauseates me as I pull my shirt over my nose. Mom's expert fingers press down organ keys, and their minor tones drone from the balcony above.

I sit with Dad at the back of church; after Mass, he exits quickly so he can light up. An hour without a cigarette is an hour too long. Grandpa sits farther up, by himself, always in the fourth pew from the front.

Dad and I bend down to kneel or genuflect every five minutes. I spring up and down easily, unlike old folks like Grandpa. I can almost hear their knees creaking and cracking as they slowly stand and sink down. Father Gavin leads us through all fourteen Stations: Jesus falls carrying the cross. Jesus speaks to the crying women and says, "Daughters of Jerusalem, weep not for me, but for yourselves and for your children." Jesus is nailed to the cross. Jesus dies on the cross.

I drank in death during the week and could not escape it on Sundays. It was all around my church, all around my parents, my grandparents. Plaques depicting the Stations hung on our stone church walls year-round. I memorized them during boring sermons. Death loomed from the side walls and in front of me, too. There, above the altar, hung the crucifix—Jesus nailed to the cross, painted "blood" streaming from his hands and feet and from his head under the crown of thorns. Every year, during Veneration of the Cross, I followed the other parishioners in a slowly moving line as we made our way to the altar to kiss the small crucifix the priest held. We kissed the nailed feet of Jesus, the priest wiping the crucifix with a white cloth after each kiss. There was a crucifix in most homes I went to—in Aunt Rosanne's house, on the kitchen wall in Grandma Hager's house, on a wall centered above the bed in Grandpa's house. I received a crucifix on the day of my First Communion, when I was eight years old.

IT WAS HARD FOR ME TO BELIEVE that an entire person, body and soul, sunk into the earth and disappeared upon death. The notion that all those people Dad buried were gone, just gone, was absurd. And why not? It was hard to believe that death was the end when the dead were always coming back to life. The

Virgin Mary appeared to small children at Lourdes and Medjugorje. Jesus rose from the dead and appeared to Mary Magdalene and the disciples on the day of his resurrection. At St. Joe's, statues of the Virgin Mary and Joseph stared down from their high perches on the sides of the altar. They stared at me from stained glass windows. Jesus, resurrected from the dead, came back at Pentecost, flames dancing on the heads of the disciples.

My belief in the afterlife was so strong that it sank into my bones and vibrated with realness. It was what my parents believed. Dad told a newspaper reporter in 1986, who interviewed him about his gravestone for a story in the *Mankato Free Press:* "[Loretta and I] were both brought up [to believe] that death is not final. The body goes into the ground, but the most important part of the body goes on." It was what their parents believed, and their parents before them. The belief was passed down to me, as genetic as the skinny fingers and blue eyes I got from Mom. A belief wound just as tightly through my DNA as my genes for height and the timbre of my voice. My inheritance.

AFTER MASS, Grandpa makes his way to his car. He walks down the church's cement front steps with his lopsided gait, his legs bowed like a cowboy's. Dad smokes yet another cigarette, talking with George and Jerry and Gerald. Mom lingers in the choir loft, gathering her music, chatting with Beth, the choir director.

Grandpa sits in the car to hurry them up, a signal that he's waiting. I join him there, opening the incredibly heavy and well-built passenger door to slip inside. Grandpa takes out the round tin of chewing tobacco from his pocket. He pinches a wad and puts it between his gum and lower lip. The sharp, minty smell tickles my nose.

"Want some *snus*?" he asks, offering the tin in my direction. He asks this question every week.

"No, thank you," I reply, just as I do every week. Grandpa takes back the tin and chuckles. It's our game.

On the drive home, equally as slow as the drive to church, his brass spittoon sits between my feet, the brownish spittle sloshing back and forth. Grandpa's back is curved, his neck craned, looking, always looking.

Church comforts the lonely, those who've lost, those who grieve. It is a weekly ritual that never changes, never goes away. You can go to Mass anywhere around the world—Waseca, North Dakota, Poland, Ireland—and the only difference would be the language. Church provides us something to cling to, the rope line tied from the barn to the house during a blizzard. No matter what swirls around you, you cannot become lost.

LONELINESS EMANATED FROM GRANDPA, but we never spoke of it. I wanted to know more about his parents, what he remembered of their deaths. I wanted to know more about his life on the North Dakota prairie with his uncle Paul and aunt Agnes, his godparents, bound by Christian duty to take him in. I wanted to know how a seven-year-old absorbed the separation from his siblings after his parents died. The older three went to an orphanage, and the youngest was adopted. But I didn't ask. To do so would be an intrusion. Grandpa's grief was his alone.

His parents are nearly lost to memory. Their shadows hang by just a thread. A wedding portrait was the only image of them that existed. We had two other portraits of Grandpa's mom, Mary—one possibly a confirmation photo, the other perhaps from high school graduation. Flat, broad eastern European cheeks, full lips, enigmatic Mona Lisa smile. I saw in her my reflection, which was a comfort. I was forever searching old family photos for evidence of myself. Some proof that I belonged here, that I came from something, a thread that connected me to this family. Her cheeks and lips were mine.

In the wedding portrait Mary and Vincent sit stiffly in chairs, far apart. He's strongly handsome, big, with a square jaw and straight, chiseled nose. She's much smaller, with rounded, soft features.

Their youth and beauty could not save them. The 1918 influenza claimed the young. The fact that they were so healthy was precisely the reason why they died. Their strong immune systems went into overdrive, flooding the body with fighter white blood cells. The cells multiplied and grouped, came together in thick white masses, filled the lungs, choked out air. Their strength was their weakness.

I FOUND MYSELF DRAWN TO GRANDPA, to his house. I went to his house almost every day in the summer to bring him his mail. I relished walking to the mailbox every morning around eleven o'clock, knowing that something from the outside world was coming to our house, a break in the isolation.

Grandpa gave a cursory glance to his mail when I handed it to him, then laid it on the coffee table to his right. I took a seat on the couch. We spoke little. But I sat for a requisite amount of time—twenty minutes, a half hour.

At other times, I went to Grandpa's house to help him shuck peas or make gooey popcorn balls at Halloween. No one else did this. Just me. We worked in silence. But the silence was so comforting that I could have stayed that way forever.

* * *

WE PILED INTO GRANDPA'S BUICK on the last day of June 1979—
Mom, Renee, and I. Grandpa parked the car in front of our
house, and Dad helped Mom load suitcases into the trunk. Dad
and Andy were staying home: Dad on the pretense that if someone died, he had to dig the grave; Andy on the pretense of keeping Dad company and not wanting to be stuck in the car with
three girls, even if Grandpa was driving.

My legs sweated on the long, hot drive, the pristine show-
room plastic on the seat imprinting small red triangles on the
backs of my thighs. I wondered if Grandpa noticed how Renee
and Andy, when they were smaller, had picked away at the thin
fabric that covered the inside roof. The spongy yellow padding
looked like cake and compelled my fingers to touch, too.

We drove for ten hours, far into North Dakota's interior,
to a town named Lansford, to visit relatives. The relation was
never made clear to me. My definition of "relatives" was people
you see all the time, like the way I saw Aunt Rosanne or my
cousin Karen a lot. But the people in North Dakota were people
I had never seen before. They had strange names like Basil and
Isadore. We stayed at Basil's house, where he lived with his
wife, Dorothy. Basil and Dorothy looked to be about Grandpa's age. A houseful of people arrived to greet us. Isadore and
his wife, Jean, were also around Grandpa's age. I heard a reference to Paul, Uncle Paul, which jumps out at me because it's
Dad's name.

Only the younger people enter my field of vision, such as
a girl named Teresa, around Renee's age. I liked her frequent
laugh and the fact that her name was my middle name. Another Paul was a boy my age, and we chased each other outside
and played with toys on the living room floor. Another woman

there, a little older than Renee, had a baby boy, whom I awkwardly held.

These North Dakota names were the names of saints— St. Isadore, St. Teresa, St. Paul. It wasn't important for me to understand who these people were, how they fit into our lives. But it seemed important for Grandpa to be here, because at home Grandpa was alone. I had my parents, my brother and sister, my overflowing abundance of aunts and uncles and cousins. But few people stopped by his house, save for us and Uncle Ray. It's as if Grandpa had been fashioned like Adam from the earth and given a directive to procreate. Grandpa presided like a king over family gatherings, the only representative of his generation. He didn't go to family reunions as I did, big, giant affairs held in Medford's city park. It's as if he had been put here to be my grandpa, nothing more before, nothing after.

Our visit here suggested a previous life, a mysterious life that had existed before me, before Renee, before Mom. This was a homecoming to the place where Grandpa had been a child, had run around this land as Paul and I now did.

OUTSIDE OF LANSFORD, I STAND IN A CEMETERY.

I skip and run around a giant, simple concrete cross. I'm four years old, and the cross dwarfs me, its shadow long in the morning light. Around me, the dozens of gravestones at this Catholic cemetery are smaller versions of this large cross. These gravestones look nothing like the ones at home: no fancy obelisks, no heavy squares of granite, no crucifixes or statues of Mary like the ones at St. Mary's in Waseca. Here, everything is simple, befitting a Great Plains state.

The wind blows strongly. With no trees to stop it for hundreds of miles, the wind races and gains strength until it meets me and whips my pigtails around my face. The spot where I stand is flat, glaciers having scraped it as precisely as a plane smooths a board. If it wasn't for the curve of the earth, I would be able to see for hundreds of miles. As it is, I can see faraway grain elevators that dot the horizon. In this place it's as though I need to make a conscious effort to stay grounded. I picture the wind transforming my sundress into a parachute and sailing me far across the prairie.

"Rachael!" Renee yells from a few yards away in the cemetery. I turn my head toward her. She holds the Polaroid camera. The camera had chronicled our trip so far, whirring and then spitting out pictures of our motel room in Jamestown, the prairie grasses, Paul and I sitting close on the recliner, the camera rendering us suddenly shy.

"Smile!" she instructs as she points the bulky camera toward me. I do as she says. My sundress threatens to rise up and reveal my underpants; I smooth it down with my hands while the sun beats on my milky-white shoulders. The camera clicks and out comes the blank photograph. I race over to my sister.

"Let me see!" I say, bouncing up and down on my toes.

"Just wait! You'll ruin it."

"No, I won't! Give it here. I know what to do."

She hands me the photograph. I grasp it by the white strip on the bottom and shake it. I watch the paper as it gives birth to watery colors that merge, blend, and swirl until forms emerge: me and the cross.

I run past gravestones and over graves, picture in hand, to where Mom and Grandpa stand. They look down on a pair of plain white crosses—no names—embedded in a slab of cement.

"Mom!" I shout. "Look at the picture Renee took!"

Mom looks at me. "Shhhh. Just wait a minute."

I look at her, look at Grandpa. Their faces are quiet, determined. I become quiet.

Grandpa holds two plastic stakes. On top of each stake is a nameplate. One says "Vincent Zimny" and the other says "Mary Zimny," each letter a small sticker, gold printing on black. Grandpa got the nameplates from Walt Kinder. Funeral directors pound these temporary markers into the ground at a freshly dug grave before a gravestone has been set. Grandpa intends these stakes to be permanent. He can't afford solid granite gravestones.

Grandpa bends over and sticks one stake into the thick dirt. He pushes down hard, wiggles it into the earth. He takes the other one and does the same thing. He straightens up, as much as his crooked back allows. He stands at the graves for a few moments. I wait, but then get impatient and run back over to Renee, who's wandering nearby.

I look back as I run, at Grandpa, his head bowed and heavy.

Dad's gravestone

Chapter 7

AS YOU THINK,
YOU TRAVEL

HIS IS INSCRIBED on the front of my parents' gravestone:

As you think, you travel; and as you love, you attract. You are today where your thoughts have brought you; you will be tomorrow where your thoughts take you. You can not escape the result of your thoughts, but you can endure and learn, can accept and be glad. You will realize the vision (not the idle wish), of your heart, be it base or beautiful, or a mixture of both, for you will always gravitate towards that which you, secretly, most love. Into your hands will be placed the exact result of your thoughts; you will receive that which you earn: no more, no less. Whatever your present environment may be, you will fall, remain, or rise with your thoughts, your vision, your ideal. You will become as small as your controlling desire; as great as your dominant aspiration.

A copy of this poem, "Ideals," written in the nineteenth century by James Lane Allen, hung for years on our bathroom wall across from the toilet. Mom had torn it out of a magazine and mounted it on the wall using Scotch tape, which became yellowed and crusted over the years. The poem first appeared on the bathroom wall in the early 1980s, when Dad and Mom got sucked into Amway, the home-based sales business that offered heavy doses of motivation along with soap, laundry detergent, and makeup.

I memorized the poem. Learning it by rote was easy when the words were placed in a spot I could not avoid. That piece of paper became part of the landscape, as much a part of the bathroom as the built-in linen closet and mirrored medicine cabinet above the sink. I couldn't grasp the meaning of this vaguely New Age–like prose. The words stood by themselves, connected in sentences yet not saying anything. But I could recite the entire poem, just as I could recite Hail Holy Queen in church at the end of the rosary without knowing what it meant.

At the surface, "Ideals" seemed to clash with our everyday lives: dirt and sweat; death; nights in front of the television, getting lost in the worlds of *The Dukes of Hazzard* and *Dallas* and *St. Elsewhere.* What right did we have to claim this poem? It was too beautiful, too dreamy, to belong to blue-collar folks with high-school educations. Beauty and culture were for others, like the doctors and bankers and car dealers who lived on Clear Lake Drive. If we were driving through Waseca at night, Mom and I would have Dad cruise slowly around the lake so we could peer into curtainless windows to glimpse grand pianos and chandeliers, to see how the other half lived.

If I had given the same intense attention to my own life, I would have seen that art was all around us, cultivated by Mom and Dad, who surrounded themselves with beauty in this tenuous world.

BILL HOLM, one of the finest writers to come out of the Minnesota prairie, says in his essay collection *The Music of*

Failure: "That house was a metaphor for the interior life that they stocked with the greatest beauty and intelligence they understood."

Dad and Mom created a beautiful space for themselves, for our entire family, a haven to which we retreated, where everything was beautiful and uplifting. Our home was a cocoon, insulating us from the reality of the everyday. Awareness of time shaped the way Dad viewed life, inspired him to collect and arrange, to control and orchestrate his corner of the world, to surround himself with what he deemed beautiful.

In the early 1980s, Dad started to collect anything depicting eagles, mainly bald eagles. Soon, Dad and Mom made the leap to fine art. I relished trips to the art store in Minneapolis because we didn't often go into the big city, which was new and exciting and filled with people. We were small-town hicks. Mom wouldn't even drive in the Cities (what Minnesotans call the Twin Cities of Minneapolis and St. Paul); the busy traffic made her nervous. At some point on each drive, Mom or Dad would watch a jet approaching or taking off from the Minneapolis–St. Paul International Airport and exclaim, "Wow! Look at that plane!" They'd crane their necks and look out the windshield at the sky instead of the road. They'd been on a plane once, to an Amway convention in Memphis in 1980.

In Minneapolis, we'd stop at Hutch and Mantle, a collectibles store on Lyndale Avenue South. At the store, I inhaled sophistication. Hutch and Mantle contained more beautiful things than I could have ever imagined existed at one place: paintings, sculptures, vases, grandfather clocks. Breakables were arranged carefully on end tables. I moved slowly; Mom seemed able to keep one eye on the paintings and one eye on me at the same time. Other people wandered around the store—people I imagined to be rich, true art connoisseurs, intellectuals, customers who truly belonged there, not poseurs. I wondered if these people dug dirt out of their fingernails every night with a metal file or cut calluses off their feet with sharp scissors, as Dad did.

Dad and Mom would consult with the owner Jan, and she'd pull out catalogs for them to browse. Clocks chiming each quarter hour sang in my ears. I looked out the large plate-glass window in front. Cars zipped by on Lyndale, and pedestrians on the sidewalk ambled past. Dad and Mom would place their order and make another trip when the order came in.

Dad and Mom carefully placed the Mario Fernandez prints on the walls, arranged the sculptures they purchased in a hutch cabinet bought just for the displays, and hung gold-plated collectible plates just so. Our living room was worthy of an art gallery: neat and refined, clean, not one thing out of place. I was not allowed to clutter this room with my toys or other junk.

And there was music, too, every day. Notes floated down the hallway from the music room at the end of the house. Mom's organ rested along one wall—the organ that she'd had as long as I could remember. To fill out the music room, Mom and Dad bought an old upright piano for twenty-five dollars from Uncle Neil and Aunt Donna and set it against another wall. Mom spent hours each week in front of her organ. She sat on the bench, her back straight, eyes focused on the music in front of her, slightly swaying from one side to the other to the beat, sometimes singing along.

When she wasn't practicing for Mass, I'd steal into the music room and sit on the bench, imitating her posture and mannerisms. That organ was a favorite toy. When I flipped the organ's switch to "on," the letters of the middle scale zapped to life and lit up underneath my fingertips. When I had just learned the alphabet, Mom carefully penciled in the letters above each note in a Christmas songbook so I could play the music. The organ's plethora of buttons and keys and levers combined to make an infinite number of sounds—some melodious, some cacophonous, some annoying and shrill. One note could sound like a flute, another like a trumpet, the next a vibrating harp. Using only the deep bass foot pedals, I could play entire songs—"Peter Peter Pumpkin Eater" and "Mary Had a Little Lamb."

Sometimes Mom would get out her violin, which she had played in high school. She was out of practice and not very good. But that she even knew how to play a violin surprised me. Violins were the provinces of symphonies and orchestras, of which Waseca had none. Here people played piano and organ, trumpet and clarinet. A violin was cultured and classy. Who was this woman? She possessed an inner sophistication. She wore perfectly accented scarves and gold hoop earrings. She subscribed to *Metropolitan Home* magazine and carefully studied the pages, sometimes tearing out glossy photos and taping them to various cupboards in the kitchen. She was from here, but not of here. The house was her domain, and she always kept it neat and elegant. She lived in the country, outside of small-town Minnesota, but in her home, she could be anyone.

Where did Mom go when she played her violin? Where did her mind wander? When the notes floated up and away, I imagine that she did, too. As you think, you travel.

ART *WAS* ALL AROUND. It surrounded us in its own midwestern way. Art was a field of corn and soybeans planted in perfectly straight rows. Art was in the church choir, with Beth Bentley, a farmer's wife, energetically leading the chorus of voices. Art was with me as I learned piano in the basement of Penny Peters's house on Tuesdays after school.

Artists in this world were not skinny, pale men wearing black turtlenecks and sunglasses, nor women in flowing skirts and scarves and wind-whipped hair. Artists were gravediggers like Paul Swenson in New Richland, who on dark winter days took rough, splintered stumps of wood and chiseled them into clocks, picture frames, and vases. Artists were Uncle Alfie, my Uncle Wayne's uncle, who seamlessly blended slivers of wood in every color into decorative plates and tucked ships into glass bottles as if by magic.

Art was gravedigging; Dad just happened to carve dirt instead of clay or marble. He matched the gravetop's sod perfectly with the grass around it, like finding the perfect color to blend in with a painting. He stepped back and viewed his work with a discerning eye, fixing and rearranging any stray grass or plucking weeds that might mar his masterpiece.

Art was on the gravestones. If Andy Warhol descended from the sky, would he see cemeteries as art? Or would he see only the work of sensible, grounded, practical midwesterners? Mom and Dad worked, came home, and cleaned up; we all ate and then retired to the living room for a night in front of the television. This wasn't a world filled with overt arts appreciation or intellectual discussions about politics and philosophy around the table. I couldn't reconcile blue-collar work with art. But there it was, stitched subtly into the landscape.

Once at Hutch and Mantle, Dad bought a piece of art for me, a small, delicate vase. The light from the window shone through the deep, ruby-red mottled glass, and sparkles danced. I picked it up and ran my fingers over the dips and rises. Jan carefully wrapped it in brown paper, and I carried it to the car as I would have carried an infant. On the way home, I continued to examine it, thrilled to have something so beautiful to call my own. At home, I put it on my desk, beginning to create my own haven of beautiful things. As you think, you travel.

THERE ARE TWO EAGLES on Dad and Mom's gravestone. One flies high at the top, above "Ideals." The other is one of three symbols next to "Paul," along with "DAD" and his logo, the cartoon man on the backhoe. Dad's need to choose his own gravestone was a need to be known. Maybe it was a by-product of being one of sixteen kids, an aversion to being one of many. Dad possessed a compulsion to stand out, to do things on his own, in his own way.

He knew he wouldn't be on this earth for long, that even if he lived to be eighty, ninety, one hundred, that's still only a blip of history. He liked to know people, and he liked to be known. He didn't create books, art, or music. His labor didn't last much beyond a few weeks—he worked at making graves neat and hoped that people *wouldn't* know he had been there. So the beauty of the gravestone was all he had, the only proof that he had walked this earth.

Grandparents Anna and Henry Hager *(right)*, with Anna's brother
Andrew Hollinger and Henry's sister Marie, May 22, 1928,
Waterville, Minnesota

Chapter 8

WHEN BEAUTY DIES

*I*F I WERE ANDY, I would have been at Corpus Christi cemetery the day Dad dug his brother Davey's grave. But I was neither old enough nor a boy. My brother was fifteen years old that summer and sported the same sandy hair and brawny build as Dad. Andy packed a force behind a shovel that I lacked. Between the two of them, they had the grave dug in less than an hour.

Dad dug most graves himself. Ordinarily this would have been a job he could have handled easily. It was a sunny July day, the sky clear and blue above. No driving rain, no snow, no thick frost in the ground to chop through. The soil at Corpus Christi was rich and silty like the Minnesota farmland that surrounded it, easy to dig, not like the rocky clay of some cemeteries. Perfect digging conditions.

Maybe Dad brought Andy because he wanted to get out of that place as quickly as possible. Here, unlike in his other cemeteries, the ground enclosed more than anonymous dead. The ground cradled family—Dad's dad, the baby sisters Mary Jean and Lucille, a stillborn nephew. Maybe Dad was afraid of ghosts. Maybe he was afraid of memories. But he also wanted to escape a place in his mind—the place where the new absence of a dead brother loomed fresh, like an open wound. When brothers die, they take a piece of you along. With Andy there, Dad could stay focused on the present. If I were Andy, would I have noticed how quietly Dad worked? He put all his concentration into Davey's grave—no talk, no rest, so unlike the casual way he dug other graves.

If I were Andy, when the grave was finished I would have helped Dad load the backhoe onto the trailer, place plywood over the hole, put green tarp over the mound of dirt, stack shovels in the back of the pickup. I would have jumped into the passenger seat as Dad started the ignition. The sound escaping from Dad's lungs like a strangled cough would have made me turn my head, and I would have seen Dad wipe his eyes and say *I'm OK, I'll be OK.*

Mork's General Store was not even a mile down the road from Corpus Christi. Did Dad plan to stop there all along? Or did he find he could drive no farther? At Mork's he'd find neighbors and friends from his days growing up on the Blooming Grove Township farm. Mork's, at the corner of two blacktop roads, straddled the line between Blooming Grove and Deerfield Townships. It straddled the line between past and present, an old-fashioned country store plopped into the late twentieth century. Mork's was where Grandma had bought sugar and flour. It was where farmers had gathered on rainy days to talk crops and weather. It was where Dad and his brothers had brought their pennies and nickels to exchange for root beer barrels and Beechnut gum. Its hardwood floors were grayed with age and dust, and tools and canned goods filled wooden shelves. A cash register from the 1930s sat on the counter, and behind the counter stood Kenny Mork. The store and everything in it was a relic, including Kenny. Kenny Mork, old and gray, wild hair, voice gravelly from cigarette after cigarette, eyes puffy from years of beer.

Kenny barely sold anything anymore. But he kept the store and lived in the house next door, unwilling to let go of the merchandise, unwilling to let go of days such as these, days in which a grown-up Hager kid would stop by with his own kid just to chat.

If I were Andy that day, I would have said *Hi* to Kenny, said *Hi* to Floyd Minske, said *Hi* to the other neighbor farmers there. I would have watched Kenny crack open a beer for Dad and pass bottles to the other men. As a teenage boy, I would have wanted one. I would have heard *Here's to Davey* as the guys lifted their bottles, brought them to their lips, and swigged the amber brew. I would have sat there as the guys shared stories about Davey, a de facto memorial service at a country store. It would be a better memorial to Davey, I would have thought, than the ritual church service sure to come.

After the guys had a few more beers, I would have stood up when Dad stood up, ready to go. What would I have thought when Dad, overcome with emotion, said *You're going to have to drive home.*

I would have looked into those watery eyes, those light-brown eyes with their strange red flecks, and searched for the joke. But there wouldn't be one. If I were Andy, I would have had only my permit and a few hours of behind-the-wheel instruction. But I would do as I was told and drive the twenty miles home. I would get into the driver's seat of the red pickup while Dad took his place to my right. I would think how strange this is, how strange it feels to be thrust so abruptly into the driver's seat. But I would start the truck and drive away. I would sneak a glance toward Dad, wonder what he was thinking as he leaned his head against the window and looked toward the old farm where he grew up.

DAD FINDS NO WORKDAY COMPLETE without at least three breaks: one in the morning, around nine o'clock; one for lunch; and one in the afternoon, around two thirty or three. On break, he drinks coffee as if he had never tasted it before and smokes cigarettes as if it were his last day. Never mind the fact that he constantly pours caffeine and nicotine into his system, whether he's on break or not. But for Dad, a personable guy with a solitary job, coffee and cigarettes taste best with others around.

At break time, we all stop work in the cemetery, and we pile into Dad's truck. I ride in the truck bed, my butt firmly anchored to the hump of the tire wheel, my hands gripping tight to the sides of the truck as Dad navigates corners. The breeze moves through my hair as we travel down Highway 14, past the stately homes, the middle school, the Lutheran church. Our destination: Busy Bee Café on Main Street.

The smell of greasy hamburgers and French fries permeates this place, a diner steeped in the 1950s, replete with Formica-topped tables surrounded by chairs with cushioned, shiny black vinyl seats, the kind that squish down slowly and let out a bit of air as you sit. Swivel chairs line the long counter, and forks and spoons and glasses constantly clink.

There are two waitresses at Busy Bee. Cheryl is the shorter of the two and, in my opinion, the prettier one. She reminds me of my Angel Face Barbie, the one who came with her own makeup compact, white lace blouse, and full pink skirt.

I watch Cheryl as she moves gracefully from table to table. She possesses the kind of beauty I see on television, a beauty generally not seen around here. Her hair is deliciously feathered and flipped, the same hair worn by Sue Ellen or Pam on *Dallas*, the same hair Farrah Fawcett wears as she gazes down from a poster on Andy's bedroom wall. Color vibrates from Cheryl's face—blue eye shadow, pink cheeks, red lips. Something pulses from within her, too. Men here sit up a little straighter when she comes around—Dad, too. They unconsciously smooth their hair and wipe their mouths with the backs of their hands to brush away crumbs. Cheryl buoys these men, men who aren't going anywhere, men who would always stay in Waseca with the same wife and the same job and travel the same roads every day to the same house. Cheryl—a young woman without wrinkles or a pot belly or sagging breasts—laughs at their jokes, touches them lightly on their shoulders, strokes their egos. Their crushes on Cheryl are contagious; I'm infatuated with her, too. Mostly I wonder, though: *Why is she here?* Beautiful women don't stay in Waseca. This town is populated with ordinary women—women with brown mousy hair teased into tight perms, jeans clinging in unflattering ways to fat deposits on hips and thighs, women trapped in jobs at Brown Printing or Birds Eye or E. F. Johnson's. If I were as beautiful as Cheryl, surely I would go away from here, maybe join the beauties in Hollywood.

But I am not beautiful. I feel destined to be ordinary. I grew out of the cute stage around age seven. I stayed adorable through kindergarten, then in first grade Mom's hairdresser wound my hair tight around rods and applied a foul-smelling solution that burned my nose. I saw my taut curls in the mirror and wanted to cry. At home Dad chanted, "Fuzzy Wuzzy was a bear, Fuzzy Wuzzy had no hair!"

The "Fuzzy" nickname stuck. My looks became a center of attention in my family, but only in a comical way. Mom

dressed me in neutrals, not the pastels that were usually reserved for girlie girls. No one ever told my parents *Oh, what
a beautiful little girl you have!* I was lucky if they could tell I
was a girl. My baby incisors had fallen out and were replaced by
a huge new pair with a large gap, two big white Chiclets front
and center.

With determination, I study beauty, as if by studying it I
could become beautiful. I flip through Renee's yearbooks until the binding starts to break loose. I memorize hairstyles and
fashion. The same pretty faces appear page after page. Does
popularity breed beauty, or is it the other way around? Renee
points out different pictures to me: *She gets invited to all the
parties. . . . She's anorexic but everyone loves her—you should
see how thin she is. . . . This girl's car is going to be used in a
scene in Prince's* Purple Rain.

I wish one day for a large chest and stilty legs, like those
of my Barbies or of Miss America contestants. I hope to one
day wear Daisy Duke shorts as well as Catherine Bach herself.
But I have the body of a child, with rolls of baby fat thanks
to a meat-and-potatoes diet supplemented by chocolate milk,
M&Ms, and Mom's buttery chocolate chip cookies.

I can't imagine Cheryl as an awkward child. In my mind,
she emerged from the womb in her present state. Even her child
is beautiful, five-year-old Dawn, a stunning doll princess with
blond hair cascading down in tight ringlets. Dawn is destined
for beauty, like her mother.

If I had a magic wand, I would transform my mousy brown
hair to Cheryl blond. I would replace my terrible perm and
smooth it into feathered waves. I would wish for my nose to
shrink to pert proportions. I would melt away my baby fat and
turn my figure into one that matches Cheryl's.

I thought that maybe I could pick up Cheryl's beauty through osmosis. So I wanted to be around her often, just like the men here.

THE NIGHT OF CHERYL AND DAWN TUTTLE'S WAKE, Dad drives our Cadillac into Waseca, Mom in the passenger seat and me in the back. It's early evening, suppertime. Streetlights flicker on as the wan March sun goes to bed in the western sky. Dad trolls for a few minutes looking for a parking space; cars hug curbs continuously on the streets surrounding Kinder Home for Funerals. We find a spot a few blocks away and walk to the funeral home; dirty snow crunches under our boots. At the front door, we tromp on the floor mat and wipe our feet. Dad goes through the heavy wooden door first, holding it open for me and Mom and a few people straggling in behind us.

Walt Kinder himself acts as doorman; his funeral home is a one-man show. The indoor lights shine off his slicked-back, jet-black hair. Somehow he keeps his tan year-round, which leads Mom to whisper periodically that he must have Indian blood. Having Indian blood is not something people around here acknowledge, but the dark skin and black hair and high cheekbones of people we know tell the truth. Kinder's tan complements the gold he wears on his fingers, wrist, and around his neck. He greets us with a muted nod, which Dad returns.

Earlier in the week, the phone rang for Dad, and he grabbed the receiver.

Hello?

Yeah, Digger, it's Kinder. Cheryl Tuttle died this morning. Her little girl, too. House fire right after Bill left for work.

Christ. Are you kidding?

No. A neighbor saw the smoke and called the fire depart-
ment. They told Bill at the bank, and he came home, but it
was too late. They were by the door. They almost made it out.
Christl. How old was she?
Twenty-four. Dawn was five.
Yeah, I thought Cheryl was pretty young. Goddamn.
So, I don't know when they'll want the funeral. I'm guess-
ing maybe Thursday. Burial somewhere at Woodville, but
they don't have plots yet. I'm meeting with Bill later this af-
ternoon, so I'll give you a call after, all right?
Yeah, OK.

Dad, Mom, and I move slowly through the mass of people
in the foyer. Almost everyone in town knew Cheryl from the
Busy Bee. And if they didn't know her, then they knew her husband, Bill.

Dad had already been to Woodville Cemetery earlier in the
day to dig the graves. They will be buried in the newer part of
Woodville, down by the garage, not too far from Uncle Harold
and Vicki.

When we get to the guest book, Dad stops to sign our names.
I reach around Dad to grab a visitation card, that piece of paper
folded like so many others with a soft forest scene printed on
the front, Cheryl's and Dawn's obituaries inside, and Psalm 23
on the back. I enter the viewing room squarely sandwiched between Dad and Mom. I'm eight years old and quickly approaching Mom's height, though I come up only to the middle of Dad's
barrel chest.

People fill the room. I've never seen Kinder's so crowded.
They flow like sand into spaces among chairs covered with
padded beige, and their feet plant into soft carpet. They speak
quietly in groups of twos and threes, words mixing together to

create one low hum. In their hands, they wring visitation cards and Kleenex into ersatz origami.

The air in funeral homes feels different from outside air. To-night, a heaviness presses down, ghostly fingers dancing on my flesh. The living emanate grief from their pores. The palpable grief thickens the air; it's like an August day in a swamp. And the bodies of Cheryl and Dawn are breaking down physically. The living and dead infuse this space with zinging, invisible currents of energy. I breathe that unseen weight into my nose and mouth, and it travels into my chest like a rock and settles in my lungs. The charge in a funeral home is a magnetic pull that either repels people or draws them in. It draws me in.

At this wake, the charged air interferes with my hearing and vision, like lightning that makes our AM car radio crackle. Voices start to grow faraway and dreamlike, including Dad's, as he glad-hands and chats with others *(Do you know how the fire started? Have you talked to Bill? How's he doing? This is just a shame; they'd only been married five months. . . . Cheryl was just the nicest thing and that daughter, gosh, what a cutie . . .).*

We inch our way forward. The people filing toward the caskets move slowly, and the line behind us soon weaves out of the visitation room, out of the foyer, out through Kinder's front door. I start to lose track of those around me. The caskets will not let me see others in the room. I see only Cheryl and Dawn, the soft funeral home lights trying to cast a glow upon their pallid faces. I float forward, holding my gaze steady on them. Dad and Mom fall away from my periphery. I sense them but cannot see them, as in my mind Cheryl and Dawn become larger and larger until they take up the entire space in the room. The three of us are the only ones here. It is just me, and death.

In the smaller casket, Dawn's blond ringlets splay out on the white pillow. Walt's wife, Edie, has a flair for doing the hair and makeup for the dead. With Dawn, Edie had tried to re-create a princess. Dawn wears the flower girl dress she had worn a few months before at her mom's wedding to Bill.

After my few quiet moments in front of Dawn, I step to my right, in front of Cheryl's casket. I come to within inches of her face, cock my head, and lean in. Death does not quell her beauty. Her hands are sculpted into a folded position on her stomach. She's wearing her wedding dress; it shimmers. She's a Victorian maiden, surrounded by the silky whites of the casket fabric. I do not smell death. I smell only sweetness from nearby bouquets. Her face is waxy and flat, but she still radiates a hint of beauty.

There's not a mark on Cheryl or Dawn. They died of smoke inhalation rather than burns. It's as if God himself did not want to mar his perfect creations. Cheryl looks no different from pictures of Sleeping Beauty in my fairy-tale books. I want to believe that's who she is, resting there quietly because she pricked her finger on a spindle. I *want* to believe the stories, just as I want to believe Vicki's picture will be different.

Dad nudges me. I look around and see that I'm holding up the line. I move on. As I walk out of the visitation room behind Mom and Dad, I turn around for a last look. That night the casket lids will close on more than just the bodies of Cheryl and Dawn.

ONE SUNDAY, like many Sunday afternoons when Mom and Dad and I went to Grandma's house to play Polish poker with her and Uncle Davey, I asked Grandma Hager about her wedding dress.

"I was wondering, do you still have your wedding dress?"
I said.

She paused. "No, I don't have that anymore," she said.
"During the Depression, we were so poor I had to cut it up to
make dresses for my little girls."

I pictured my aunts Loretta and Helen as young children,
romping around in new Sunday-best dresses. But that wasn't
what she meant.

IN A SMALL FARMHOUSE just north of Waseca, in August 1933,
my father's mother looks into her closet. She stares at the few
clothes in that small space. A Sunday dress and work dresses.
The work dresses were plain cotton calico with tiny faded pat-
terns, flowers and checkers. Lots of red and blue, durable and
well-suited to farmwork and housework. Her dress pattern had
just two variations—with sleeves for fall, winter, and spring,
and sleeveless for summer. She purposely made the dresses
large; they billowed around her petite frame. That way, she
didn't have to make new clothes each time she was pregnant—
four times already in five years of marriage. She sewed big
pockets into the dresses, hiding places for eggs, washcloths,
clothespins. For her girls she made similar smocks.

Anna fingers the cotton dresses. *These will just not work,*
she thinks. She sits on the bed to think. What could she use?
She couldn't buy new fabric. She couldn't use her Sunday dress
to make a burial gown for Lucille. She needs that dress to look
proper herself at the funeral.

LUCILLE WAS ALREADY SICK and getting sicker when Mary Jean
was born in June. Anna held the newborn close to her chest

that day and asked the nurse, "What about Mary Jean? Lucille is coughing so badly and has a high temperature at home. Will this baby be all right? Won't she get sick, too?"

The nurse fluffed Anna's pillow behind her back. "Oh, you have nothing to worry about, Mrs. Hager. The baby will be just fine. You'll be breastfeeding her. That gives babies a natural immunity. She'll be strong and healthy, you just watch." The nurse winked and smiled.

Anna nodded as the nurse left the room. She could trust nurses, couldn't she? She looked down at Mary Jean, touched her soft cheek with a finger. These nurses went to school. They knew about such things. What did Anna know? She was just a farm wife, twenty-six years old.

But others worried, too. When Anna brought Mary Jean home, neighbors Rose and Mary stopped by with food and an offer.

"Why don't you let me take the baby for a while, Anna," Rose said. "I don't think it's good that such a little one be around that bad cough."

Mary nodded. "I agree. Let Rose take her for just a few weeks. She'll be right next door. You can come by whenever you want." Mary put the canned food they had brought into the pantry. "That way, you can stay home and concentrate on Lucille, help her get better."

Anna smoothed back her hair; the humidity created wayward frizzes that framed her face. "No, I don't think that'll be necessary. The nurses said Mary Jean would be just fine. I'd rather keep her here with me. I'd miss her so if she were gone."

SHE TOOK IN A RAGGED BREATH. So much to do—plan a funeral, take care of baby Mary Jean, and somehow sew a little dress out of something.

Maybe one of her sisters had something she could borrow. But her sisters were poor, too, and she would feel bad if she were to take something nice that belonged to someone else. She had to have something, there had to be something in the closet she could use, maybe a scrap left over from a sewing project. She got up and looked into the closet again. She shuffled her fingers through the dresses, moving the hangers to the right as she mentally cataloged them. She shoved the utilitarian dresses to one side and reached back to the dark recesses. Her fingers touched light, smooth, cool fabric. Her wedding dress.

She took the hanger off the closet rod and looked closely at the gown. She pressed the material smooth. Anna held the dress to her nose and inhaled. Could she do it? Could she cut up her wedding dress? She quickly put it back onto its hanger and hung it in the closet. No, there had to be something else. This was a family heirloom. What would she have to pass down to her daughters?

She sat back down on the bed. She eyed the closet, locked in a showdown with it. The dresses within seemed to be taunting her. A voice echoed in her head: *What else is there? There's nothing else you can use.*

Anna rose up, slowly. She reached into the closet and grabbed the wedding dress. She draped it over an arm and walked downstairs to her sewing machine. She spread out the dress on the table and took shears from her sewing basket. A big breath before the first cut. Her hand with the shears seemed poised above the dress for minutes, hours.

Then, the first cut. After that, the cuts came more quickly, strongly, until she had enough pieces to sew together. She fashioned little sleeves and a collar. She told herself she was making a Sunday dress, just a Sunday dress, for her baby. The second she thought about it as a funeral dress, tears slipped down her cheeks and onto the fabric.

* * *

THEN, IN OCTOBER, when Mary Jean died, Anna took out the amputated dress from the drawer she had placed it in two months before. She had kept it, the material too valuable to throw away. She thought she could use it for baptismal gowns, or even little pillows or keepsakes to pass down to her daughters in lieu of a complete dress. She had secretly hoped, too, that maybe she could salvage the dress, put it back together if she ever found the perfect replacement swatch.

But now she was sewing a second funeral dress. She cut a smaller swath this time, just big enough to swaddle a three-month-old baby.

St. Jarlath's Church in rural Waseca County

Chapter 9

A GOSSAMER WORLD

*M*OM DRIVES THE CAR TO ST. JARLATH'S, where we'll meet Dad and the mowers already parked there. We head north out of Waseca on County Road 5, the road snaking and undulating through creek-carved hills.

Just outside Waseca, we follow the blacktop's curve that turns sharply to the west. I wonder what would happen if once, just once, Mom didn't follow the curve and instead drove straight ahead on a little-used gravel road. What if, just once, we parked the car by the patch of trees so thick they appear black? What would it be like to walk through the dark woods where the bad things happened? Would I feel the evil? Would it sink into my blood, my bones? A part of me wants to take the dare. Another part of me wants to stay far, very far, away.

We drive past, and the trees retreat in the side mirror. As surely as I want to hear again about what happened in those woods long ago, Mom is surely happy to tell me. I don't know when I first heard the story of the Schuch murders. It's as if it were sewn into the quilt of my subconscious, as if Mom whispered the details while I slept in her womb. I knew about the Schuchs the same way I had always known about Santa Claus or Jesus—never seen, but there nonetheless, a constant story, a presence shaped by Mom and her words.

I look down at my lap, to the books that will keep me company while Mom and Dad work.

"What happened in those woods, again?" I ask. "What about the Schuchs?"

I bite my lip as soon as I speak. Is this the time Mom tires of telling the story? I fear her saying *That again? You already know about all that.* I try to space out my questions every few weeks, usually adding an excuse like *I don't remember what exactly happened* or *What year was that again?*

Mom takes a breath. Her eyes stay focused on the road. But there's a nearly imperceptible narrowing of the eyes, a glint that suggests Mom relishes retelling a good story. Luckily for me, she begins. I exhale and settle into my seat.

"It was during the Depression," she says, looking ahead. "Julius Schuch lived there in the woods with his kids. His wife had just died. One Saturday night, a couple of people broke into the house. They heard he kept a bunch of money in a safe, that he was a tight German farmer. He put up a fight, of course, so the guys killed him. They also killed his two kids, a little girl and boy. Didn't want any witnesses, I guess. Bludgeoned them to death with a hammer or something like it. There was blood everywhere."

That's all the detail I need for grainy film footage to sputter to life in my mind. I first see a ramshackle farmhouse, flaking white paint exposing naked wood underneath. Then, focusing on the house, a lean-to porch, leading to a simple kitchen with white ceramic appliances. A couple of guys knock at the door, shadowy figures, their backs to my eye. I see Julius walking through the kitchen, the kids playing by the stairs, wondering who could be visiting so late. The thieves surprise Julius;

he struggles against them and manages to break free. He runs out of the house and yells to the children *Run, hurry, get help*. Eda, the girl, does not move. Her mouth gapes open, and she's paralyzed with fear. The boy, though, runs after his dad. In my vision, the murderers grin wickedly as they chase down and kill first Julius, then the boy. Tracking back to the house for the safe, they find Eda still there and kill her, too. The movie in my mind fades to black, just after I see the Schuchs lying in blood.

For a brief moment, I am there.

Quiet spots in and around Waseca belie their dark pasts. Cemeteries were not simply granite and grass, woods were not simply trees, and houses were not simply siding and windows. If you looked deeper, you'd find a story. If you dug, you'd uncover evil.

THE PROXIMITY OF THE SCHUCH WOODS to St. Jarlath's contributed to the overall darkness of the cemetery, a few miles northwest of Waseca. If you believe old wives and Stephen King, places can have a "shine." To me, each cemetery had a distinct personality and hummed with its own vibe. If Woodville were a person, it would be the life of the party, hip and modern and popular. Calvary, on the other side of town, was quiet and spiritual, like a nun. But just as there were people I didn't like— Nikki Schaal on my school bus with her heavy eye makeup and sneering disposition—there were cemeteries I didn't like, either, cemeteries I couldn't wait to leave. St. Jarlath's was one of them.

The area's Irish settlers named the church after a sixth-century Irish bishop who was said to kneel in prayer three hundred times a day and three hundred times a night. St. Jarlath was also blessed with the gift of prophecy, the ability to see through shadows and peer into the future.

For one hundred years, the Iosco Township Irish and their descendants attended Mass at St. Jarlath's each Sunday and holy days of obligation. But by the late 1960s, the rural population had dwindled. Those who remained in the country easily drove their cars the few miles into Waseca for Mass at Sacred Heart. The diocese closed St. Jarlath's in 1968, but the church remained. By the time we started mowing the cemetery, paint had shed off the church's exterior walls, and broken windows looked like missing teeth. I wished I could go inside.

One day, as I walked around the church and came to the front, I saw that the door—usually locked tight—stood ajar. I stared for a long moment, then looked around. Dad was trimming; Mom was mowing. I wanted to go inside, but not by myself. I waited until Mom finished mowing. As Dad loaded the mowers onto the trailer, I led Mom to the church. She was just as curious as I.

Mom opened the door farther; it was heavier than she anticipated, and she had to tug hard. We slipped inside to a tiny narthex, big enough for only about five people. Then we pushed on the swinging wooden doors that opened into the sanctuary. The squeak of old wood echoed in the church.

The inside appeared abruptly abandoned, as if the Rapture had occurred and we weren't among the chosen. A slightly yellowed calendar tacked to a bulletin board in the back was stuck on October 1968. Hymnals were still stacked at the ends of pews. Tiny mouse tooth marks punctured the wooden baseboards. Mom and I walked down the aisle, turned around, and peered up at the organ in the balcony.

"Can we go up there?" I asked.

Mom shook her head. "I don't think so. The wood up there is old. It might not be safe."

We continued toward the front of the church and walked through a doorway to the left of the altar, over which a giant crucifix, Jesus bloody and dead, hung. We entered a small kitchen, and Mom opened up the cupboards.

She gasped. "Oh, look at these," she whispered, pulling out a couple of porcelain plates and turning them over in her hands. "I can't believe they just left these here."

The past and present collided in many places, but no place so jarringly as at St. Jarlath's. Where we stood, invisible parishioners from bygone days walked among us, through us. Around us, women bustled in tea-length skirts, white gloves, and hats. Outside, men in suit coats and ties and children scrubbed clean with neatly parted hair waited patiently for ham sandwiches, coffee, and juice. The line here between life and death was very thin indeed. Dizziness washed over me, a sensation of floating between two worlds.

The church also situated itself between two times, past and present. Standing in front of the church, looking to its left, I could see the newer gravestones of the recently departed that held surnames of my classmates—Haley, Pfeiffer, Androli. To the right were the old marble gravestones, weathered and falling over, pitched at odd angles, a clichéd horror-movie scene. Those buried here were relatives of those on the other side of the church, ancestors who had come from Ireland to this fertile place. Big oaks filled the old part of the cemetery. Grass grew in erratic patches, failing to thrive in the spotty sunlight. When I stood in the old section, I could have been anywhere—Waseca County or Ireland. I could have been in 1860 or now. For a split second, I truly didn't know where I was.

An eerie silence permeated this place. A little-used road ran past the cemetery, which sat on top of a slight knoll. This was lake and creek country with grand vistas and dips and rises. Waseca County is on the fringes of the Big Woods; the flat prairie of the Great Plains doesn't start for another forty miles to the west. You'd think the top of a hill would catch the wind, that the breeze would flutter through trees and sing a song, but at St. Jarlath's, leaves didn't move and birds didn't sing. It's as if creatures avoided this place, just as animals are said to avoid the remains of Holocaust death camps. Even Dad's trimmer and the mowers sounded muffled and far away.

MOM HAD ANOTHER STORY ABOUT THIS PLACE, TOO.

Sheriff Eustice is buried at St. Jarlath's, in the back. I didn't like going to the back of the cemetery. The air became darker and heavier as I walked alongside the church in the shadows of the eaves, next to broken windows and a chipped stone foundation. The branches of thick oaks interlaced like fingers over my head. The hard, new tombstones up front gave way to soft marbles spotted with moss and age. I forced myself back there each time, addicted to the coursing of adrenaline that fear pumped through my veins, just as I went outside each time a thunderstorm approached—scared to be outside, yet too engrossed by the shifting, dark clouds to look away.

The sheriff's headstone beamed like a diamond next to the dullness of century-old marble around him. Sheriff Eustice himself beckoned me—his picture smiled from the gravestone. At forty-two, his hair was already gray, but his eyes were bright. The collar of his brown uniform peeked from the bottom of the picture. Surely his was a story that I needed to know.

Sheriff Eustice was gunned down on duty in 1976. He drove

out to a farmstead near the cemetery on a September morning to serve commitment papers to a man he knew. Both the man, Kenny Jewison, and Eustice had grown up in the area, their families going back a couple of generations; you can find the first immigrant Jewisons and Eustices buried near each other at St. Jarlath's. Eustice greeted the man on the porch—*Hi, Kenny*—and explained why he was there, that Jewison's family was concerned, that it would be in the best interest of his mental health to be locked up for a while. In one swift motion, Kenny grabbed a shotgun resting on the porch, aimed it, and killed the sheriff with one shot.

Mom added the details. Our neighbor on Wilton River Road, Mert Schwartz, was with Sheriff Eustice that day. I knew Mert, a former deputy, a tall, white-haired guy with a stable of horses.

"Mert expected to receive Kenny's next shot," Mom said. "But Kenny told him, 'I'm not going to shoot you, Mert. We're friends.'"

Connections like Mert Schwartz were everywhere. People who were there, who witnessed the stories as they happened or their aftermaths, like Aunt Margaret who had gone to the Zimmerman wake.

Mom had more to add to the Schuch story. "You know your Uncle Wayne's uncle, Uncle Alfie?"

I nodded. "He's the one who makes all those wood carvings?" I asked, thinking of the beautiful plate Mom displayed in the living room, a plate intricately crafted by the hands of an old German farmer from slivers of different-colored wood—oak and pine, maple and cedar.

"Yes, that's Uncle Alfie. Anyway, he used to live around here. He was living here when the Schuchs were murdered, and he heard the screams that night. Thought it was a wild animal, a coyote maybe. He never thought to check on his neighbors."

Someone I knew was nearby that night. One degree of separation, a thin thread of a spider's web, linked me to the past, to the ugliness that was buried everywhere, even in places that appeared serene.

I filed away Sheriff Eustice's story with the stories of the Schuchs and the Zimmermans. Like the other stories, there was more to this one than simple facts. Each time I stood in front of the sheriff's gravestone, in front of his picture, I understood that no one was invincible. Not even a sheriff, strong and sworn to serve and protect. The strongest man I knew was my dad. Certainly the sheriff's three daughters looked at their dad the same way I viewed mine. Did Becky, Peggy, and Barbara Eustice fold their little hands into his, the way Dad's calloused and thick fingers wound around mine when we crossed the street or walked through the county fair? Did the sheriff laugh a big, hearty laugh when they said something funny? Did they wrap their arms around his neck the way I clung to my dad? Dad carried me in his arms even when I was far too big to be there, at five or six already tall and gangly, because I was afraid of Aunt Rosanne's nipping dogs. I clasped my fingers around his neck, safely held up away from the danger, and wished I could stay that way forever.

St. Jarlath's was filled with other strong men, Irish immigrants who were strong enough to survive famine in their country, board a ship, steam for weeks across the ocean, disembark, and trek halfway across a continent. Men who came here, broke the land, and cut down acres of trees with handsaws. Men who sweated until they thought they could sweat no more, men who couldn't feel their toes when blizzards struck. Men who pulled wet, squirming calves from wailing cows and guided heavy plows behind horses. The same men whose strong backs also carried their daughters and whose hands grasped tiny fingers.

Dad was strong, too. His arms grew solid and thick from the literally tons of dirt he'd hefted over the years. Our house, our Cadillac, our comfortable way of life, was built on his back. He was our Atlas, carrying us into the future.

In the back of St. Jarlath's, among the trees, the world revealed itself to be like gossamer. We were connected to it on nothing but whisper-thin strings, strong yet vulnerable. In one unexpected moment, they can break. They snap, and we float away.

MY FAVORITE BOOKSHELF in the Hartley Elementary School library was the one on the south wall. Go through the main doors, turn right, and walk all the way down to the end of the room. This was where I stumbled across the 100s, the Dewey decimal numbers for the occult, the paranormal, the unexplained, and there I became anchored. In school, I learned about the concrete: math equations that always had right and wrong answers and scientific facts that never wavered—Earth was 75 percent water, trees breathed in the carbon dioxide we breathed out, and how the body's five senses worked. But my mind wandered. The Romantics rebelled against science, and so did I. I longed to learn more about what we *couldn't* see. My body buzzed with a sense that the things around me I could not see were *right there,* at any moment ready to break into my world. And I had to be prepared when they did.

I came home with books on werewolves, Bigfoot, UFOs, ESP stuffed into my backpack alongside textbooks. I became like a scientist searching for evidence, an amateur detective, a young Nancy Drew, searching for clues. I picked up every book on the Hartley shelf that spoke to spooky encounters. Spirits that roamed old hotels, farmhouses, ships. Spirits that talked and threw things, spirits that brought along with them a cold draft in an otherwise warm room. Gentle spirits, evil spirits.

More than anything, I wanted to see a ghost for myself. The thought thrilled and frightened me at the same time. I wanted spirits to appear to me, I wanted the possibility that something would disrupt the placid calm, but if it actually manifested I would will it away with all my might. So I played Bloody Mary with my cousins, but always chickened out before chanting the third "Bloody Mary" in front of the mirror. I placed my fingers under cousins lying on the floor and repeated "light as a feather, stiff as a board," but I pulled away before anything could happen.

I wanted supernatural visits from those who had passed on. But I never got them. Did I lack a gift so many others seemed to have? I grew up with stories of Marian visits to poor children in places with exotic names such as Lourdes and Medjugorje. Why did the Virgin choose those children, and not me? What made them so special? If I knew there was a secret ingredient, I would have done anything in my power to grab it.

My cousin Karen insisted that her mom saw ghosts. I believed her. Aunt Linda, in her soft-spoken way, emanated something mysterious and enigmatic. She could take one look at a woman's bulging belly and declare "boy" or "girl." And she'd be right.

"Mom saw Grandma Zimny a few nights after she died," Karen said one day as we sat on the bed in her cluttered bedroom, only the narrowest path of blue shag carpet peeking out from amid the toys showered on her by her other grandma.

"Really?" I asked. "What did she see?"

"Grandma came into the bedroom. Mom woke up and saw her standing at the foot of the bed."

I pictured Grandma the way that I remembered her, wearing a calico housedress and her glasses. I imagined that Grandma floated before Aunt Linda, shimmering and smiling.

"Did Grandma say anything?" I asked.

"I dunno," Karen said, shrugging her shoulders. "I don't think so."

I wondered why Grandma would come to Aunt Linda. Maybe Aunt Linda was the only one of us who had the "gift," the ability to peer into that other world. Maybe Grandma knew that Aunt Linda was the only one who could receive. But if there was a message from the other side, Karen didn't elaborate. Even though I was curious, I didn't ask Aunt Linda about the apparition. This, too, seemed like a family secret, a story that wouldn't or shouldn't be told. And there was a small part of me that thought perhaps it wasn't true. There was a possibility that it was a joke on Aunt Linda's part, something she would tell a gullible child. I so wanted it to be true that I didn't want to risk the chance of finding out otherwise. In my mind, it happened. A story like the ones I was reading, but it happened right here in the house in which I stood.

In my bedroom at night, I prayed that I would see a ghost—a friendly one, of course. One like Grandma or the Virgin Mary, kind and full of peace. How incredible it would be to talk to someone who had died, to continue a conversation, to chat about things as if nothing had happened. Death would no longer be a barrier, an end to all communication.

There was a way you could talk to the dead. All you needed was a portal, a type of spiritual telephone. Karen had a Ouija board. Mom wouldn't let me have one; she said it would invite evil inside our home. Part of me believed her, and deep down I was relieved we couldn't have one in the house. *Poltergeist* had just come out, and I envisioned my bedroom closet glowing with a tunnel to a dark world. I wanted to play with a Ouija board but preferably one that belonged to someone else.

So on nights that I stayed at Karen's, we brought out the board. By this time, Karen had created a room for herself in the cement-floor basement. Uncle Ray had laid down a twenty-by-twenty-foot piece of scrap carpet and put up a couple of wall dividers. She had her own little corner in the musty, spider-filled basement. We tried to make the room as eerie as possible: we lit candles and shut off the lights. We balanced the Ouija board on our knees, gently touched our fingertips to the pointer. We asked warm-up questions: *Does Mike like me? Yes. Yes! Are we in Karen's house?* A quick *Yes.* And then, always the question *Who are you?* And then we held our breath. Who are you? What spirit is guiding the oracle? What kind of answer would we get?

Usually we wouldn't get much—the pointer didn't move or it spelled out a string of random letters. But one night, we got an answer. For a while, the pointer didn't move. We sat on the blue carpet and waited. Then, slowly, the pointer started to spell, one letter after another. My heart was pounding; Karen's, too.

N-O-R-B-E-R-T.

Our dead uncle. The one that no one spoke of. He had lived on this land where we sat, in a different house, where Karen's house now stood.

Our fingers flew off the pointer, and we looked at each other. "All right, that's enough for me," Karen said shakily, moving the board off our laps. I never moved the pointer that time, or in all the years I played. Because I believed the Ouija worked. I believed that something, somehow, could magically spell out answers from the other side. Maybe Karen knew my unwavering faith in the board and wanted to fool me. But the look in her eyes that night would be hard to fake.

We went upstairs to where Ray and Linda were watching television, a room with lights and other people, a room without shadowy dark corners or Ouija boards that spelled the name of a dead uncle.

EVEN WITH THE SPOOKY HAPPENINGS, I took comfort in knowing this otherworldly realm existed. When I found the Dewey decimal 100s, a wave of relief washed over me. The books verified my idea of unseen presences, something with heft and dimension yet invisible, something that physics could not explain. I *did* feel something in the cemeteries and funeral homes. Others felt it, too, in other places. Spirits *did* exist.

The books gave weight to what I already sensed: that another world existed in conjunction with ours, a world populated by spirits, a world that we acknowledged at Mass, where we prayed to the dead. We prayed for spirits to guide us, to intercede for us, to pull our dead relatives out of purgatory and push them into heaven. It was a mysterious, magical world, a world in which the dead really were not dead. They were always coming back to life, resurrecting, reappearing.

The progression of childhood reading, from Mother Goose to *Helter Skelter*

Chapter 10

HELTER SKELTER

*A*SUMMER DAY, LIKE ANY OTHER. The door opens, and Dad walks into the house. I can't see him from the living room, where I'm watching television. But I know his moves; they're the same every day. He pauses in the entry-way and takes off his heavy Red Wing work boots. Then, into the kitchen where he stops at the refrigerator, digs through his pants pockets, and clears out the front pocket of his shirt. Loose change jingles. He sets the coins on top of the refrigerator, along with a lighter, his pocket watch, and whatever is left in his pack of cigarettes.

But this summer day in 1986 is different from the others. I hear the words "Lloyd Quesenberry" and "girlfriend" and "dead" that Dad directs to Mom, who's in the kitchen preparing supper. I know her moves too; they're the same every day. She unwraps a cut of red meat from its brown paper, thin trails of watery blood dripping into the yellow ceramic sink.

Mom says, "What?" I stop listening to the television.

Lloyd Quesenberry is a young funeral director who came to town a few months ago. Lloyd is often at the café in Janes-ville, a small town ten miles west of us on Highway 14, where we usually stop after a morning of mowing the two cemeteries on the outskirts of the town. Dad and Mom shake dice with Lloyd, the small-town ritual that determines which of the group pays for the round of coffee. While they shake dice, I watch. I watch Lloyd. He's not as friendly as Kinder or Sandberg. Lloyd has never talked to me, aside from a perfunctory "hello" when we first met. I don't try to speak to him, either. Whereas Sandberg and Kinder are slight, Lloyd is broad-shouldered and intimidating.

Dad says Lorraine died last night at the apartment she shared with Lloyd in Janesville. Lloyd told police officers that she had a heart attack.

I want to know more, but I'm afraid Dad might leave out juicy details if I come into the kitchen. So I pretend not to care and turn my attention back to the television. I couldn't see that Mom likely raised her eyebrows. She may have said, "Don't you remember what Lloyd said the other day at the café?" To which Dad may have said, "No."

"He was so mad at Lorraine. I forget why, but he was mad. Then he said, 'I could just kill her.' You don't remember that?"

"No. I must have been talking to someone else."

"Well, that's what he said. I heard it loud and clear." She pauses, rinses the meat. "Do you think I should tell the cops about that? It gave me the creeps."

"Nah, just leave it be. If something did happen, if she didn't have a heart attack, they'll figure it out."

Whatever truth Dad and Mom may have suspected comes out a couple of days later. When the police arrived at Lloyd and Lorraine's apartment, when they reached down to pick up her body, they noticed a dark purpling creeping across her face. When they touched her corpse, they could feel broken ribs and other bones. Lloyd's story quickly changed from *must have been a heart attack* to *oh yes, now I remember, she fell down the stairs.* Pushed down the stairs was more like it. Lloyd, with his morphing story, was promptly arrested. Our town buzzes with the news that the funeral director beat his girlfriend to death. I try to absorb the fact that a man I knew, a man that Mom knew, a man that Dad knew and worked with, was a murderer. His hands were responsible for death.

Then a week later, another murder. This one, too, in Janesville. Mona Armendariz, a young mother, was knifed to death in her trailer park bedroom by a teen crazed on drugs. Janesville is a town of only 1,800, and two murders within a week force people to pay attention. I read about the murders in newspapers that Dad brings home every morning—the *Minneapolis Star and Tribune*, the *Mankato Free Press*, the *Waseca County News*, and the *Waseca Journal*. Pictures of Janesville are splashed across the pages. At night, before we go to bed, we watch the Twin Cities news stations. The reporters stand in front of the Janesville café, the café where men threaten violence with a roll of the dice.

I WAS ELEVEN THAT SUMMER. Even before the murders the year had shown its darkness. The space shuttle *Challenger* exploded in January. We had been following the launch closely as fifth-graders because of the teacher onboard, Christa McAuliffe. That night, I couldn't stop watching the news. Over and over, I saw the shuttle take off, only to see seventy-three seconds later the white vapor trail give birth to two branches, trails of smoke and debris descending to the ground. I was watching people die. Then in April, the Chernobyl disaster. On television, we watched a time-lapse predicted progression of the radiation cloud across Europe. Would we also fall, poisoned and sick?

Until this year, stories of crime and disaster had been con-
fined to graveyards, rising up only when channeled through
Mom. But Mom's stories, as morbid and tragic as they were,
lived safely in the past and were about people I didn't know.
Now death was occurring in random, spectacular ways—the
Challenger and the Janesville murders, the death cloud hanging
over Chernobyl—and the present became brutal, too. Tragedy
emerged from the shadows of the past and became a mist that
crossed into my reality.

The stories had broken the surly bonds of graveyard gates.
No safety bubble enveloped my town, my family. There was
no special place, no fallout shelter, that would protect me or
my family from death. I decided it was only a matter of time
before that mist found me, too, like it found Lorraine, like it
found Mona, the Schuchs, Sheriff Eustice, like it found Christa
McAuliffe and the other astronauts. At the age of eleven, I real-
ized my halcyon days were numbered.

I BEGAN A QUEST for contemporary stories of death, ones I could
read for myself, ones that Mom could not filter. Always a dedi-
cated reader, my appetite for the words of true stories became
voracious. The summer of 1986 had been a rebirth of sorts, and
I came out of it hungry for stories, a newborn hungry for food.
Books, which had always been my trusted companions, became
almost necessary, as essential as water or air. They became necessary to fill in the gaps; I needed to learn everything about the
world and its inherent dangers. Mom and Dad were willing to
show me only so much.

At a time when my classmates were passing around the
middle school library's only dog-eared copy of *A Wrinkle in
Time* with its fairy-tale flying centaur on the cover, or the girls

underlined passages in *Are You There, God? It's Me, Margaret*, I was reading about people who left this world suddenly, brutally early, seeking to find a rhyme or reason to the randomness. I became a student of death. Gritty, true-life stories of people in peril drew me in. Stories that reflected this world. It was as if this harshness took form, shook me by the shoulders, and forced me to open my eyes and face the truth. To live in a land of fairy tales, of fiction, would be the easy, but cowardly, way out.

At an estate sale, I discovered a copy of *Helter Skelter*, its cover tattered and worn. I grabbed it off a table while Mom and Dad wandered a nameless lady's house in Waseca. Strangers picked through this woman's earthly possessions, and her furniture and appliances were sold at bargain prices. I thumbed through the book's pages, so worn that they were smooth. Inside the front cover, where "25 cents" was scrawled in pencil, these words screamed out in bold print: "The story you are about to read will scare the hell out of you." I nearly trembled with anticipation.

I turned to the pictures inside, photos of wild-eyed and bushy-haired Charles Manson, his devoted young followers, and the crime scenes. For publication, the bodies were excised from the police photos, leaving big chunks of white space in the form of people. The beautiful Sharon Tate, one of Manson's first victims, was nothing more than an outline filled in with white. Still, I could tell she was sprawled in front of a couch, one arm over her head. She lay on her side, and the roundness of what had been an eight-month pregnancy clearly protruded.

Mom walked by as I held the book. I quickly closed the cover on the gruesome photos, showed the book to her, and said, "Can I get this? It's only a quarter." She barely glanced over and nodded, distracted by a pink chair she wanted for our living room. I got the book home and promptly read the entire thing.

* * *

RENEE AND I shared a small room in my family's double-wide trailer house until I was about six or seven. Renee had inherited Mom's love of books. Renee kept the books she was currently reading on a small end table by the bed. One day when she was out of the room, I picked up her latest read. I held the heavy, hardcover book with a plastic library dustjacket in my hands. I'm not sure if I was able to read at that time—if I could, I couldn't read very well. I was turning the book in my hands, about to flip through the pages, when Renee came into the room.

"Don't look at that," she said, snatching it out of my hands.

"Why not?" I asked.

"The pictures will give you nightmares."

"Why? What's it about?"

Renee told me the story of Ed Gein, the Wisconsin farmer who was arrested in 1957 after police found women's body parts in his home and buried on his land.

"He made lampshades out of women's skin," Renee said.

The gruesome image stuck in my head, and the fear of nightmares kept me away from the book until Renee returned it to the library.

When we drove past our cemeteries at night on the way home, our headlights glinted off gravestones. "Ed Gein's platter," Dad would say, and I shuddered.

MY FIRST TASTE OF DEATH ON THE PAGE was *Bridge to Terabithia*, and I thought I had found my soul mate in Jess Aarons. As I read, I felt a familiar hum in my head, and the words vibrated within me. Until then, my literary world had existed of solvable mysteries, clever, titian-haired Nancy Drew putting the pieces together every time. Or the cute antics of Ramona Quimby or the bizarre life of Pippi Longstocking. Funny books, books with happy endings neatly tied in a bow.

But in *Bridge to Terabithia*, I found a kid so real he could have jumped off the page and into my life. He was a person my age who also knew death and went to a wake, where a roomful of grief threatened to swallow him but he refused to succumb: "He looked around the room full of red-eyed adults. *Look at me*, he wanted to say to them. *I'm not crying.*"

My family went to wakes like some families went to movies. Waseca was a small town. Everyone was a family member, a neighbor, a relative of a neighbor, a friend of a friend, a teller at the bank, a waitress at the café. I think part of Dad, too, wanted to show up and offer his sympathy, provide the face of the gravedigger. His presence said he wasn't out to make a buck, wasn't out to just do a job. He was a member of this community, too.

Other people my age also went to wakes—we were all part of this small town. But no one went as much as I. No one spent their summer days in cemeteries, though occasionally my friend, Amy, came with me, and we rode our three-speed bikes up and down cemetery roads. I didn't feel the need to talk about my immersion in death; I didn't feel a heavy pressing on my chest that had to get out. People here didn't show much emotion; we didn't pour out our love or sadness. These were people of periods, not exclamation points. If I couldn't connect with people in person, I could connect with them on the page.

I knew death, but *Bridge to Terabithia* showed me grief, the part of the story others left out. I learned what could happen to the people left behind. At wakes I caught only glimpses of grief, those initial moments of shock that render family as zombies.

Immediate grief forms a quiet, hard surface that makes it impossible to peer inside. Quiet tears slipped down cheeks, of course, and there were gentle hugs, but the calm surface of a sea hides volatile riptides flowing beneath.

The murders of 1986 made the gap between *Bridge to Terabithia* and *Helter Skelter* very small indeed. The summer, with its violent deaths, demanded a book on the scale of *Helter Skelter.*

In our house, it was entirely appropriate for an eleven-year-old to read *Helter Skelter.* Mom's nonreaction at the estate sale proved I had no need to hide it, no need to read it furtively by flashlight like it was some type of pornography. I read it out in the open, in a chair in the living room while everyone else watched television. Mom valued a good story; she wasn't going to stop me.

I wanted to know more about men like Manson, like Lloyd, like Mona's killer. When I finished *Helter Skelter,* I moved on to other crime stories. At bookstores, I headed straight to the true-crime section. I scanned the shelves, reading book titles spine by spine. I chose books about the Boston Strangler, Son of Sam, the Zodiac killer, and Ted Bundy. I handed them to Mom, who paid for them at the front counter. The stories filled my nights.

When I was about thirteen, I came across the Ed Gein book that Renee had warned me about so long ago. But now I was older, wiser. I could handle gruesome. I was ready for these pictures.

But I was not. They were not edited for publication like in *Helter Skelter.* All was on display. The human skin lampshades. The skulls on bed posts. And the one I remember most clearly, a pair of woman's legs, skinned, raw meat hanging from what looked like a clothesline. Like one would hang a deer carcass for processing. A wave of nausea gripped me, and I ran from the store.

THE JANESVILLE MURDERS seemed to open a portal in my universe, where I recalled every violent story Mom ever told me: the Schuchs, the sheriff, my school's speech therapist who had been viciously beaten and left for dead in the woods. "Her face swelled so badly they didn't even recognize her," Mom said. When pretty Mrs. Lyons helped me shape my "S" into a crisp, sharp sound, I wondered if her bronzer, bright blush, and blue eye shadow helped to cover scars.

Helter Skelter was my entry into a world of crime and violence. I read with fascination about the hippies who convened at Manson's commune. The girls who ended up there seemed so much older than me, but in reality, some were just fourteen or fifteen years old—runaways looking for a haven. Why would they run away? I couldn't fathom hating my family so much that I had to escape.

I could see the evil in Manson's eyes in that famous, crazed photo. I stared at the photo, training myself to recognize that look. That would be a look to run away from, not run to. If I ever saw that look on anyone, I would know to run away. I would stay safe. Did Lloyd have that look? What about Mona's killer? If only they had trained themselves to recognize that look, like I was doing, maybe they could have saved themselves.

READING BECAME A PROTECTION; the words were a blanket I wrapped tightly around me. The stories helped me prepare for the inevitable. I surrounded myself with these words, reminders that bad things happen to good people. I read somewhere that we are drawn to stories of death and disease to convince ourselves that we would act differently. That somehow, by learning of someone else's story, we can protect ourselves. I will recognize the look of a crazed man bent on murder. I will eat well and exercise in an effort to stave off diabetes, cancer, or stroke. I will not walk alone in the dark at night, nor will I make out with a guy in a car on a dead-end road. I will do it differently.

If I knew about death, the many ways to die, then I wouldn't be caught off guard. Each crime story I collected added to a wall of defense. I was building the Great Wall of China around myself. When death finally found me behind the wall and touched my family, my question wouldn't be *Why?* It would be *What took you so long?*

Family portrait, summer 1989, Waseca. *In front:* Andy, Dad, and me.
Standing: John, Mom, and Renee (holding Sean).

Chapter 11

OPENING NIGHT

*D*AD ASKS MOM TO BRING THE CAR to the back of the house. He can no longer bear the pain in his stomach, and he doesn't think he can walk the fifty feet to the garage.

Mom pulls the car onto the back lawn, just a few feet from the door. She walks up the steps to get Dad. He leans heavily on her, hobbling down the steps one by one. I had been waiting with him in our entryway, and there I stand as he slowly makes his way to the car. Mom eases him into the passenger seat. I've never seen him dependent; he looks so small. After just a few moments, I have to turn my head away because this isn't the dad I know. Also what I don't know: this is the last time I would see him walk, the second-to-last time I'd see him lucid, and the last time he'll be home.

We don't speak. No *Good-bye,* no *I love you.* I silently watch him go. I tell myself he won't be gone long, that he'll get to the Waseca hospital and the doctors will diagnose a urinary tract infection or something equally treatable. After a few days of antibiotics, he'll be digging graves again. At this time, there's no reason to think that he won't return home, no reason to think the story will turn out the way it actually did.

But an unease gnaws me as I watch Mom back up the car to the driveway and pull forward, gravel crunching under the weight of tires. I think, just briefly, that this is the moment I've been waiting for, the moment that I suspected would arrive at any time. I stay at the window, watching the car become smaller and smaller as it progresses toward Waseca on County Road 4, eventually disappearing into the horizon.

AT AGE FORTY-SIX, Dad gets sick and dies within three days, possibly the world's fastest case of cancer. All three days are mixed up in my mind, pieces of a jigsaw puzzle still in the box. From Waseca, Dad is taken to St. Marys Hospital in Rochester. Mom and I follow the ambulance there. We're allowed to see him in the emergency room. In the hospital bed, under bright lights, he writhes in pain. They've taken out his partial denture, so he grimaces in toothless pain. "It hurts so much," he cries. His eyes are wild, like those of a mortally wounded deer. I turn my head away, bury it in Mom's shoulder like a little girl instead of the fifteen-year-old I am. She puts her arm around me. My stomach lurches, the room spins.

That night, Mom and I stay in a dumpy tenement-like hotel across from the hospital. Dad goes into surgery. "It might be a colon obstruction," the doctor tells Mom and me as we sit side by side in his office. "We might have to take part of it out, do a colostomy. He might need a bag. But we won't be sure until we get in."

Surgeons slice a knife through Dad's soft belly skin. When they dig in, they see ugly growths all over his insides, riddled throughout the organ linings. The cancer had sprouted a complex root system impossible to cut out. Even these doctors at St. Marys—part of the famous Mayo family of hospitals—cannot fix this, cannot deftly carve out the cancer. There's no way to make this body neat again. The cancer had suffocated all function as easily as a pillow over a mouth. All the doctors can do is close him up and wait for him to die. He doesn't wake up.

Mom requests a priest. Dad's post-op room contains nothing. No colors, just grays. No flowers, no television. Completely lifeless, a hospital purgatory. Nothing welcoming and warm, because we won't be staying, nor will Dad. He's on his movable hospital bed, ready for easy transport to the morgue. A gentle light over a nearby sink casts an eerie, yellowish glow on him.

Dad's organs are failing. Toxins start to flood his system, leaving his body massively swollen and purple. The poisons bloat his face and render him nearly unrecognizable. Death hovers near. If the Grim Reaper were real, he'd be right here, scythe at the ready, bony finger beckoning.

Mom, Renee, Andy, and I surround Dad as the priest delivers Last Rites. We perform a laying-on-of-hands on Dad's body as the priest directs us to do. I don't want to go near Dad; I don't want to touch him. What if I place too much pressure on his tender skin pulled tight like a sausage and it splits? I choose to stay far from his face, away from the swollen visage that is my dad, yet at the same time is not. I place my fingertips on him, gently, at an ankle, and repeat the ritual words after the priest. We all mumble in a daze. Dad hangs on a few more minutes, then dies.

"Who should I call?" Andy asks Mom in the hospital lobby. By this he means which funeral director should he call, Kinder or Sandberg? Mom and Dad have talked about this. Should something happen to either of them, they can declare allegiance to only one of Waseca's two funeral directors and hope the other one doesn't feel too bad about the decision.

"Kinder," Mom says, without hesitation.

IT'S AFTER TWO IN THE MORNING by the time we leave the hospital. We've been awake for hours, days it seems. Andy drives in the dark toward home. I drift to sleep around Owatonna. Twenty minutes later, just outside of Waseca, something stirs me awake. I look to my right; Calvary Cemetery's gates rush past. I can hear Dad's voice in my head: *Look, Rachael— Ed Gein's platter* as our headlights reflect off gravestones. We're about six miles from home. Even though it's the heart of the night, it's not black. I can see the road, the corn, and houses in the distance. Mom says in a hoarse whisper, "Look at that." Her head turns up, to the left. I follow her gaze. A full, engorged moon, dulled by a humid haze. I don't think I've ever seen it so large. I also know that I've never seen it that color before: bright orange, a pumpkin in the sky.

We don't speak of it, but we're all thinking the same thing: orange was Dad's favorite color.

Once home, Andy pulls the car into the garage and shuts off the engine. I wearily open the car door, as if it's too heavy for me. Into the grayish predawn I follow Mom and Andy, floating ahead of me like ghosts. The air is thick, and already birds have started their morning chatter in our pine trees, maples, and oaks. If Dad were home, he would already be up, a pot of coffee brewing in the kitchen.

If people could have seen us, we would have looked like shock victims—pale, eyes dull as if in a trance. Andy's shoulders slump, and he brings a hand to his eyes. Mom shuffles up the steps into the house, and Andy and I fall in step behind. In our entryway, I take off my shoes. Andy doesn't stop. He keeps walking straight ahead. He doesn't look back, doesn't say anything, just retreats down the basement steps to his bedroom. I watch him descend—first his legs, his back, then his head disappears. Mom goes into the kitchen, and I hear water running from the tap. I go into the bathroom, pee, and brush my teeth.

When I come out, Mom walks past in the hallway, and I follow her. She walks straight into her bedroom, and I turn left into mine. In my doorway, I turn around and look back at her. I don't remember now—was I going to say something? Maybe I take a sharp inhale and open my mouth. Or do I just watch her, looking for a cue on what to do next? What do you do the night your dad dies? What words do you speak? I need a guide, an instruction manual. I'm lost without having something in writing from which I can derive meaning.

Without glancing at me, Mom shuts the bedroom door behind her. I flinch as the door shuts into place. Neither she nor Dad ever closed their door. In our house, bedroom doors stayed wide open through the night. Growing up, in my room kitty-corner from theirs, if I woke in the night I could hear voices on their radio, tuned to WCCO, clear and bright. But now, I take her lead and shut my door, too. I crawl into bed, pull the covers up, and fall into a light sleep.

THAT WAS THE BEGINNING OF THE FRACTURE. That first night, we retreated into separate worlds. The break wasn't immediate or dramatic, not like the shattering of a snow globe falling on a wooden floor. Instead, it was a tiny windshield crack, webbing out, growing over time. Our emotions were sodden clay, waiting to be given shape, fired, and dried. That night they dried separately, and there would be no going back.

The things that happened in the quiet of a home were things I did not see in my years in the cemetery. I thought I knew death. But I didn't really *know* it; I had only created a Romantic definition of it through words and pictures. I knew nothing about the visceral side of death. In reality, the essence of death was huge, chaotic, impossible to grasp. Dad and Mom did their best to keep it at bay because the chaos of death can swallow you whole if you allow it. Dad was always in control: every blade of grass in place, the perfect way in which he dug and closed his graves, even buying his own gravestone, mulling over the choices, making it uniquely his. Then there were the careful orchestrations of Kinder and Sandberg, the neat procession of mourners at the funeral home, the coiffed hair and pink tones of the dead. The absence of natural light in the funeral home, allowing the funeral *director* complete control of how the dead would look. At Mass a similar staging, the theatrics of communion, the rehearsed lines to tame the chaos of the spiritual world. It was artifice, and we were the actors. But after the play, when the wigs came off, then what? What did the actors truly look like? What was the true face of grief?

There were clues that hinted at how big death was. It was so huge and ugly that we feared confrontation. It was the Goliath from whom everyone runs away. My family didn't talk about death or those we loved who had died. I could have known in the way that I saw those who grieve move on quickly, without publicly looking back. Once I met one of Sheriff Eustice's daughters. She sold refreshments at the many farm auctions of the 1980s that Dad and Mom attended. At one auction, I got a hot dog with Dad and Mom, and the daughter easily chatted and laughed with them. Later, when Mom told me she was the daughter of the sheriff buried at St. Jarlath's, I couldn't believe it. She had laughed so easily, her eyes crinkling at the corners, just ten years after her dad had been murdered.

I had never heard of the word "depression." I never knew what despair looked like. Those I knew who grieved must have felt depressed, must have felt despair, but it was not visible; it remained behind closed doors. No one acknowledged the possibility that grief could completely shatter a soul. I had never heard of an antidepressant, and I'd never heard of anyone going to therapy. If those things did happen, they were the quietest secrets of all. What I did know: Silence. Isolation. Grief was a burden to bear by yourself.

I wondered what would have happened if Mom had caught my eye when I looked at her from my bedroom doorway, when our emotions were yet malleable, when our new family dynamic was in its genesis. I wondered how differently the story would have turned out. When we first walked into the house, I could have sat in our entryway and cried. That would have forced Mom and Andy to pay attention. Or I could have said exactly what I was thinking: *I'm scared. What's going to happen now?*

But I remained silent. To speak up didn't seem to be my job. I wasn't our family's leader; I was the youngest. Our leader was dead. So to whom did it fall? I don't think it was a matter of someone not wanting to take the lead role. I think no one actually knew how. We were all understudies who hadn't prepared.

THE WAKE IS AN OPEN CASKET. I wish it were not. But in this town, everyone gets a traditional wake, everyone is displayed in a casket for all to view. Only the victims of the most gruesome accidents get a closed casket.

Before the wake starts, during the private family time, I walk alone up to Dad's body. He's dressed in his Sunday-best dark blue suit, white dress shirt, tie. Underneath, he's wearing his Minnesota Twins boxer shorts. He's leaving the world as Paul Hager; the suit is not something that Digger O'Dell would have worn.

Dad's face and neck are still bloated and tight. Kinder has tried to hide the purple of the skin, but a dark tinge creeps through the pancake makeup. I tilt my head, squint my eyes, and try to see the dad that I know. There will be no photographs from this wake. But there will always be this picture in my mind. I looked at him briefly, probably the least amount of time I'd ever spent in front of a casket. Still, the image will always be seared on my brain, as if by the hot sting of a branding iron.

People swarm to Kinder's on this warm Sunday evening. The stream of people through the doors and into the receiving line never ebbs. The Hagers alone—all of Dad's brothers and sisters, their kids, his own multitude of cousins—would keep this place full all night. At times, it's as if the entire town has gathered here.

Joe Ross, Dad's coffee-drinking buddy and good friend, moves through the receiving line, from Mom to Renee to Andy. By the time he gets to me, tears stream from his eyes and he can barely talk. He squeaks out, "Rachael, I'm . . . " but his voice catches, and he can no longer speak. I hug him awkwardly, want to tell him it's OK, it will be OK. This is the first time I've seen a grown man cry.

I think of Jess Aarons in *Bridge to Terabithia*. The way he saw the adults crying at Leslie's wake and wanted to say, "Look at me. I'm not crying." Jess was in control. I am in control. Or is it fear that keeps me from crying? Tonight, I'm surrounded by the sudden appearance of everything that thus far had been absent. The reality of death—Dad discolored and dead, ugly. The air swells with emotion, tears and crying, and raw sadness. I'd never been submersed in so much grief for so long. New worlds crack open, reveal themselves. But I look into them only briefly. If I cry, I will enter those worlds. And if I do, I fear that

I will drown. The shift from fairy tale to reality, from beauty to ugliness, is too abrupt. After Joe Ross, I shut down and don't let anyone in.

When I was fifteen, I thought grief was only black or white. Either you had to pretend you weren't grieving at all, or you felt grief so deeply that you became psychotic. If I let a tear slip, I would be deemed fragile, crazy, someone to be pitied, out of control. Someone lacking the fortitude to control her emotions. I didn't want to be that person. I wanted to be like the others I had watched over the years. They were strong and resilient, and I admired them.

But you can't escape without any scars. Some are visible and obvious—the tears, the depression, the shell-shocked gaze. Others are tiny, barely visible, tucked in secret places away from the eyes of the world. Mine is a story of tiny scars.

A STUDY IN NUMBERS *(because sometimes even words don't make sense):*

16: The number of birthstones in Grandma's necklace, one for each of her children. At a wedding anniversary party, her kids presented Grandma with a mother's ring, and Grandpa got a birthstone tie tack. After Grandpa died, Grandma made the tie tack into a necklace and never took it off.

1: The diamond birthstone for Dad. An April birthday, the only one out of sixteen. This white glint caught the light and sparkled amid the color. It stood out and set itself apart.

12, 7, 5: At the wake, Grandma stood near the feet of her twelfth child, her seventh son, her fifth child to die before her. That last number put as a fraction: one-third of her children preceded her in death. At Kinder's, she wore her signature white slacks and pink blouse, and she clutched a white wicker-like purse reminiscent of Queen Elizabeth or Sophia from *The Golden Girls.*

83: Grandma's age. She stood the entire time, hours, as hundreds of people filtered through the room. The way Grandma cried was not loud or demonstrative or emotional. Her blue eyes became almost translucent because tears had washed the color away.

15: My age when Dad died.

22: Andy's age.

24: Renee's age.

46: Mom's age. She knew him longer than Renee, Andy, or I. She had the most memories. Do not more memories equate to deeper grief?

1-2-3-4-5: The pecking order in the receiving line at the wake: Grandma, Mom, Renee, Andy, me. It was a hierarchy of loss with me at the end. To me, the line was a physical representation of who had the right to grieve the most, and who should grieve the least.

2: The number of parents that Grandpa Zimny had lost by the time he was seven.

6: The number of Jim Zimmerman's children who died in one day.

0: Reasons for self-pity.

I constantly measured my grief against that of others. Why should my grief be deeper than Grandma's? Than Grandpa's? The bereaved that I knew faced life with joy and gratitude rather than despair. Any time I felt the heaviness of sadness drape over me, I thought of the numbers and shrugged it off. The years in the cemeteries shaped me in many ways but probably in no way greater than by giving me a frame of reference, a sense of what had come before me. The idea that I wasn't alone, that I was not the only one who had ever grieved. It takes a village to raise a child, and my village was the graveyard.

IN MY CLOSET, COLORS WHIRL BEFORE MY EYES. My clothes overwhelm me today, and I'm paralyzed; I have no idea what to wear to Dad's funeral. I've pulled out a black skirt—a good start. But I own no black shirts. My wardrobe is decidedly vibrant, thanks to Mom. She went to one of those color consultants once, those women who looked at your skin tone and held up swatches of colored fabric next to your skin to see what hues offer the best complement. Mom returned home and said she had been classified as "warm," which meant she could wear turquoise, brown, and tan. She declared that I, with my pale, pale skin and hair recently dyed platinum blond, was "cool." My palette of clothes was the complete opposite of hers. I filled my closet with bold, striped sweaters in primary colors and jeans in fuchsia and purple.

I pick through my clothes, shoving hangers from one side to another. The most muted blouse I find is a faux silk shirt the color of faded raspberries, neat black pinstripes running down its length. But still, the color. I call for Mom. She comes into my bedroom.

"Do you think this is too bright?" I ask, holding it next to the black skirt.

Mom makes a fast assessment. "No, that'll be fine," she says, returning to her own closet.

A splash of color, then, for Dad's funeral. I pull on the skirt, button the blouse. Looking at myself in the mirror, I'm reminded of the time I wore a pink dress for my First Communion while all the other girls wore white.

* * *

AT THE VISITATION before the service, I approach the casket again. This is the last time I will see Dad. He's dead, I know, and he doesn't look like himself, but part of me wants him to stay on display, a physical crutch I can lean on. I steel myself against the idea of never seeing him again. In a week I'll try to fool myself, telling myself that he's only on a fishing trip and will be home soon. At the casket I inhale deeply, and my breath comes out jagged and hard.

I turn around and slide into a pew to my right. Stragglers come in, people who weren't at the wake the night before. The organ drones from above. This is a show for the understudies. Jeralyn Kalis replaces Mom at the organ, while Paul Swenson, Dad's coffee buddy and fellow gravedigger from New Richland, waits at the cemetery.

Renee sits in the pew behind me. She's alone. Her husband, John, must be taking care of baby Sean. Renee sniffles and brings a tissue to her nose. The hymn "On Eagles Wings" wafts from the balcony:

And He will raise you up on eagles' wings
Bear you on the breath of dawn
Make you to shine like the sun
And hold you in the palm of His hand

I shift sideways in the pew and look back at Renee.

"This was Dad's favorite song," I say. I couldn't think of anything else to say. Reaching out is so awkward and forced.

Renee barely nods and remains mute. She doesn't look at me. I feel like an intruder into her private world, as though she resents the fact that I even sat near her. This is not a new feeling. Renee is nine years older than me, and I've mostly played the role of annoying little sister throughout my life. There hasn't been much to share between us because we have little in common—she's a wife and mother, I'm just into my teens. But does it have to be this way today? My attempts at reaching out are pathetic. The little I've tried hasn't worked. We're in our own little bubbles, under our personal domes. No one can reach out and touch me.

But Mom breaks through, as moms tend to do. In the narthex, where we line up for the processional after everyone is seated for the funeral service, Mom grabs my hand and squeezes it, hard. She doesn't ease her grip as we walk slowly down the aisle, all eyes on us. This public display surprises me. Dad was more open in private, letting tears fall in front of Andy, revealing his heavy heart to me at the dining room table just months before, but Mom has always been the Great Silent One. While others talked, she remained quiet, always a friendly but mercurial Mona Lisa smile dancing on her lips, concealing her true thoughts. How she felt at losing a brother, a mother, even her husband, I could only imagine. She would never tell. I wonder if she's gripping my hand for my sake, or for hers.

AT THE CEMETERY, I sit on a folding chair at the graveside, under a maroon tent that shields the sun. Cousins, aunts, uncles, neighbors, friends surround me. I can barely breathe. I want to cry like Michelle did, but I know everyone will be watching, and I don't want pity, not like the pity I had for Michelle.

Why do I feel panicked now that I am at his graveside? Dad had buried hundreds, probably more than a thousand. I had watched dozens of burials; I had helped bury others, throwing weak shovelfuls of dirt over the vault and packing down the dirt. I had solemnly placed casket sprays on fresh mounds. I know this is where bodies go when their time on Earth is over. That's fine for others, but not for my dad. He's not supposed to actually go into the ground. It's too dark for him down there. Too suffocating. Today, Dad's casket is front and center for all to see. A pretty, classic oak, just as he had always planned, with some roses on top and a ribbon woven around them that says, "Dad."

Today, it's another gravedigger's turn to be invisible. Swenson hides among the trees in the back of the cemetery by the tool shed. He knows that I can see him, because I know where to look. I see the blue of Swenson's pickup and him inside the cab, waiting for all of us to leave. And he will follow protocol, not starting his job until we leave for the church basement and eat ham sandwiches and dessert bars. He'll bury Dad, his coffee buddy, in the quiet, the birds singing their songs on this bright and hot day. He'll breathe in and out, timing his breath with the breath of the earth, mopping the sweat of his brow with a hanky. He'll leave no tracks, no sign that he was here. Quickly (you'd be surprised at how quickly), the seams of Dad's grave will repair themselves and blend with the rest of the grass.

Zimny First Communion. From left: great-grandfather Vincent, his sister Hattie, his brother Ignatius (Andrew), and great-great-grandfather Martin.

Chapter 12

THE LORD GIVETH AND
THE LORD TAKETH AWAY

HEN I'M ALONE AT HOME, I walk into Dad and Mom's closet, where Dad's clothes still hang. In the closet, work shirts, polos, and Dockers wait limply for Dad to return and slip into them. I stand in front of the clothes and let myself fall forward. Their heft catches me and props me up. I bury my face into fabric arms and legs, inhaling the remnants of Old Spice, soap, and cigarettes. I breathe in his scent and exhale tears. The bulk of the clothes keeps me from falling, and I sag there, limp but breathing deeply, as if I could sculpt him just through a smell. I cling to the only physical part of him that remains.

Sometimes the clothes seem like the *only* things that remain. The house is quiet without Dad, only the television providing a dull background sound track to our lives. But the silence that permeates is strange. Not a single word about Dad escapes from the lips of Mom or Andy or me. I wonder what would happen if we spoke his name. Would the mere mention of it drive us over the precipice, a sure descent into madness? It's as if we fear invoking his name, afraid of what a wisp of memory could conjure. Human history is filled with names that cannot be spoken. People too lowly to speak the great name of God, people too scared to tempt the devil. To give death a name would make it too real.

Dad's absence is the elephant in the room. If we ignore it, maybe it will get up and walk away. But if his absence fades, so will our memories of him. Without any mention of him, it's as if he never existed. Speaking about him would prove that he had walked this earth. He deserves that much—a memory, a story. Instead, I'm left to wonder if he'd been just a dream.

I harbor the stories of others who bore loss. But where's Dad's story? My story? They are the domain of others, just as Jim Zimmerman and Sheriff Eustice and the Schuchs were my stories. In other households, in front of other children, perhaps Dad lives on. A drive through the cemetery, another family, another curious child who, upon seeing the giant black granite in Woodville's northeast corner and the short life carved on it, asks *What happened?* And a mother who says *Let me tell you.*

ON A HOT DAY that same July of Dad's death, I'm in my room packing. I throw shorts, T-shirts, and a swimsuit into my suitcase, and on top, a notebook for writing and a book to read. My saxophone sits in its case by my door. I'm going to band camp for a week. I've never been away from home by myself for so long, and I can't wait to leave.

I had been signed up for band camp for a few months, and after Dad died, Mom and I did not discuss the possibility of not going. A part of me wonders if going away right now is appropriate. It seems like such a normal thing to do at a time when everything is decidedly not normal. But the alternative to not going is staying home. Here I'd be stuck, eight miles from town, away from my friends, still too young for a driver's license. This house teeters as if missing a stone in the foundation. I'm dizzy, uncertain. Away from here, maybe I can regain balance.

The truth is, I'm excited to go, though I keep that to myself. My friend, Jolene, went to the camp last year and wooed me with tales of late nights and cute boys.

Mom stands in my doorway. "Are you ready?"

"Yeah, just a second." I look around to see if I've forgotten anything. My camera is on my dresser. Before I pack it away, I aim it at the open suitcase and snap a picture. I'm going somewhere for the first time, by myself. The photo tells a story of leaving.

If I could have, I would have left the confines of band camp and kept going: west, east, north, south, it wouldn't have mattered. I had my suitcase and essentials. If I had been a few years older, I might not have returned home. I wanted to find an escape, a way to leave, even though physically I was stuck.

In the spring of 1992, I was cast in the Stage Manager role in the Waseca High School production of *Our Town*. Prior to this, my sole theatrical performance had been an extra in period costume in *Phantom of the Opera*. I don't find it a coincidence that my first major stage role was in a play whose third act takes place in a cemetery. I also don't think it odd that my first role was such a large one. I had been steeped in history and harbored a love of the past; I had an unusual attachment to and awareness of those who had gone before me. I didn't just recognize Thornton Wilder's symbols of the watch and the passing trains; I felt them, lived them, saw them for myself—our chiming grandfather clock, the train tracks across the blacktop road from Woodville. I saw Waseca in Grover's Corners. The people buried in cemeteries were not just names; they were neighbors and friends with narratives attached to them. In Grover's Corners, they were Mrs. Gibbs and Mr. Stimson, the organist, and

"Editor Webb's boy, Wallace, whose appendix burst while he was on a Boy Scout trip to Crawford Notch." In Waseca, they were Sheriff Don Eustice, Mrs. Zimmerman and her children, and Uncle Harold.

I had observed stellar acting all those years. People who didn't know how well they were able to hide their true selves in order to put on a different face for the public. Dad didn't know how good he was. He didn't realize how well he had created a character to inhabit. After all, he had borrowed Digger O'Dell from radio and television and played that role to comic relief. Why? For the same reasons I wanted to take on a new role. The reality of life can be too heavy. Midwesterners are good at speaking the lines they think people want to hear, of putting on an act they think people want to see.

ON A SUMMER DAY a year after Dad died, Mom brought home a list of houses for sale. I was eating lunch at the dining room table when she passed the papers to Andy. She showed him house after house, and they talked about things such as location and square footage and yard size. No one asked my opinion. I put down my fork.

"Are we moving?" I asked.

"Yes," Mom said.

My stomach dropped. But I stayed quiet, even though I wanted to scream. *Don't take me from this house. Don't take me away from this place where Dad still exists.* The stale air that still reeked of cigarette smoke. His office, and everything in it, smelled of pipe tobacco, which he had stored in a cabinet even though he hadn't smoked a pipe for years. The small cement pad in front of our house, our basketball court, where I played H-O-R-S-E with Dad, and sometimes P-I-G when he tired of my boundless girl energy.

Mom was running to save herself, to try to save us. We moved from the country house to outrun memories. Within a month of Mom coming home with those listings, we were gone. Andy stayed behind; the house was now his. Within a year we went from a family of five to a family of two, from a country setting to the unfamiliar buzz of town life with cars and semis rumbling past on Highway 14, just a block away. Mom and I moved into a quaint brick house in town, not far from Clear Lake. The distance between the two homes was only eight physical miles, but we were transposed to a different life. If running from the past worked for Mom, I took her cue and made it work for me, too. Mom and I now operated on a different stage, where we could be different characters. The backdrop was the town of Waseca instead of barns and silos and the open spaces of cemeteries. A new supporting cast formed— for me, family exited and a new family of friends entered; for Mom, a new supporting cast of dates. Our move made it easy for me to think that a different Rachael had lived in the country, that it was a different Rachael who had loved and lost a dad.

The demarcation between the two lives was clear. But in the process of leaving ghosts behind, I also had to leave behind some of the living. All my life I had been rooted in history. The absence of reflection on the past could not last. It would creep up like grass that refuses to be buried by cement and sprouts in sidewalk cracks.

I BELIEVED what my horoscope books said about Scorpios:

> On a daily basis, you battle with a darker side where the mood swings tend to swallow you. However, with enviable determination you usually overcome them to do what you have to do and do it well. Deep inside there is a hunger that has made you

search for activities with greater meaning. You have a keen memory and a probing mind that restlessly seeks a broader understanding of the universe, and certainly of yourself.

The problems that would make another person fall apart and throw up his hands, you face with calm, poise, dignity, and a sense of self-possession. Any self-doubts you keep on the inside, while on the outside you are willful, tenacious, and exert a formidable influence in all of your undertakings. Your unusual qualities of endurance and perseverance and your strength of mind can take you through any crisis and help you grow in the unfolding of new emotional situations.

That *was* me, I determined. I proudly reread the lines, over and over. I was in control. I was not like others who crumbled in the face of emotion. I was not Michelle at the graveside. I was steadfast and strong. No one would look at me and see a young woman not in control. I would not be pitied; no one would feel sorry for me.

After a time, you become what you believe.

WHAT MIGHT OTHER NEW AGE BOOKS TELL ME? I moved away from my true-crime obsession and back to books about the otherworld. I felt restless in my quest to understand the workings of the universe. From my very inception, it seems, I had been trying to grasp this thing called death. I'm determined to uncover the mysteries of the world. Mysteries like where is Dad now. I know he's out there, somewhere. I believe in an afterlife, that the soul lives on. My belief is innate, genetic, passed down from one generation of Catholics to another. To not believe would violate my every cell. Since Dad is out there, I should be able to find him. Linda saw Grandma Zimny, and

Uncle Norbert came through the Ouija board. For years, I've been reading stories of people who have communed with the dead. I set out to do the same.

One night, I dream that I'm on a school bus, and suddenly I'm aware that I'm dreaming. "Move your arms," I think, and I do. Before I can do anything more, I wake up. I learn that I had a lucid dream, and I think maybe this is the threshold I'm looking to cross. If I can tell myself *Move your arms*, perhaps I can tell myself *Go find Dad*. In a dream world, we can meet. All I need is a portal through which to slip. So I scan the New Age section in bookstores. When I find a book I like, I plop down onto the floor, sit cross-legged, and read. I go home with books on ESP, intuition, and dreams. I truly expect Dad to appear at the foot of my bed some night.

I buy the book *Lucid Dreams in 30 Days.* But I'm impatient, as the *Sun Sign Personality Guide* says of Scorpios: "In general, you feel more comfortable in the contemplation of any action than in its execution, and tend to fantasize a lot about how you would like life to be, rather than doing something about it." I read about the silly exercises I'm to do to prep myself for lucidity, but I want to dream from the first night. When instant results elude me, I put the book away. I turn to ESP books and half-heartedly attempt to develop psychic powers, but those don't appear, either. I receive no ghostly visits from Dad, no communications. And when Dad does not come back to me in the way that I demand, I give up.

He did come back, though, through words, just like all the dead before him—through words on gravestones, through words of stories spoken. Words about him were destined to come out.

For me, he emerged in silent words in the pages of my journal. Words and story were what I was taught, my storytelling impulse filtered down through Mom. Our own stories were not to tell, at least not out loud. But I could preserve and remember without letting anyone know that I routinely traveled between past and present through the portal of my journal.

Writing let something loose in me. It gave a home to thoughts that might have devastated me if they had been trapped in my mind. Without words—the words of gravestones, the words of oral stories, the ritual words of Mass—my world was chaotic, nebulous, impossible to understand. Words had always given it a shape, shrunk it down into something I could hold in my hand.

I SETTLE INTO THE PADDED KNEELER on Grandpa's left side. Grandpa chooses the same seat every Sunday: left-hand side, fourth pew from the front. Mom is in the balcony, getting the organ music in order. Andy is at home, sleeping; he uses the house only as a crash pad. He's fallen away from the church, as has Renee.

All the years before, all those Sundays, Dad and we kids sat in the back, just ahead of the rows with parents and their babies. These days I sit with Grandpa. He never invited me to sit with him. I just found myself next to him, responding to a silent siren song. We kneel, our elbows nearly touching. I was drawn to his side, two ends of a magnet that click. We were two people who lost their moorings early. Next to him, I was in no danger of going adrift. I think the effect was the same on him, that I was keeping him anchored. The prayers help us understand each other. We never speak of this; instead, we direct our words heavenward and place our grief on Mary and Jesus and God. They're the mediators, our connection to each other and our connection to those who have died.

I look around and see there are only about ten of us here; it's a half hour before Mass. We're the faithful, the devoted. We're here to pray the rosary. Grandpa has prayed it every Sunday for decades, and who knows how many times in his home, where it's been quiet for twelve years since Grandma died. I revel in the rosary's methodical prayers, the words that never change from Sunday to Sunday. It is a template that hems me in and keeps me from going outside the lines. It's a constancy that I desire. It's Grandpa's constancy, too.

I turn my head to the left, toward a statue of the Virgin Mary, the fingers of her right hand touching her exposed, bleeding heart. Underneath her, votive candles flicker in remembrance of the sick and the dead. Grandpa's stirring to my right catches the corner of my eye. I turn to see him pull a black velvet pouch from his suit coat pocket, and, with slightly shaky hands, he loosens the black rosary beads. The rosary unfurls into the palm of his left hand. I lean back and take from my purse the plastic box that holds my cheap, white rosary. With a click, it opens and the beads cascade out freely.

We still have a couple of minutes before prayers begin. Grandpa takes the rosary's crucifix and brings it to his lips. He closes his eyes, bows his head, clasps his hands, the rosary entwined around his fingers. I do the same, though I'm not sure what I should be praying about.

Ruth Sonnek, a short woman who resembles a beach ball because she's as wide as she is tall, leads the rosary this morning. Ruth starts with the Apostle's Creed, then three Our Fathers and a Glory Be. We repeat after her. Grandpa and I mirror each other. Same pale blue eyes, those eyes with persistent eastern European dark circles underneath no matter how much sleep we get. Our lips move with the same words throughout each of the five mysteries. My fingers, elegant piano fingers like Mom's, move the beads along to keep track of where I am; Grandpa's fingers, gnarled like old tree branches, do the same.

After twenty minutes of repetitious Hail Marys, we end with the Hail Holy Queen. The church fills with quiet chanting: "To thee do we cry, poor banished children of Eve. To thee do we send up our sighs, mourning and weeping in this vale of tears." I follow along by rote. I don't know what "banished" means, and I don't know what a "vale" is, but I speak the words anyway.

"I THINK IT WOULD BE A GOOD IDEA if you moved out," Mom said.

It was early June; I had just graduated from Waseca High. My plan was to move out in September and head to the University of Minnesota in Minneapolis. But tension had filled the void Dad left behind. Mom and I clung to others, not to each other. I was dating a guy Mom didn't like—a guy with long hair, no ambition, a pot smoker. Mom was dating Terry, a devout Catholic widower who lived in Minneapolis.

It was as if seeing each other was an ever-present reminder of loss. Our minds constantly compared this new life to what we once had, and it didn't measure up. The cognitive dissonance was too much to bear. I was Mom's last dependent. When I could be on my own, so could she. She had one foot in the old world of Waseca, one foot in the new of Minneapolis. It's as if we were both adolescent girls on the cusp of new things.

I left without a fuss, because I also was eager to start anew. During high school I got used to being on my own. Nights were all mine as Mom worked the second shift at E. F. Johnson. Weekends were all mine, too. When Mom wasn't working, she was with Terry in Minneapolis. So at eighteen, I felt ready to leave. I took my six hundred dollars in graduation money, and within a week I had secured an apartment in northeast Minneapolis. Renee got me a summer job at the moving company where she worked. Only years later did Renee tell me that Mom had called her when I was moving out. *Will you help her get a job? Will you watch her, make sure she's OK?* I wore skirts and nylons and filed all day long. I was on my own sooner than I had expected.

MY BODY DESIRED to fold into another. I had been this way since I was young, craving affection as much as I craved certain foods. At times it was intense, obsessive. It was as if I needed to negate the everyday loss I absorbed in the cemeteries by imagining the hot blood of a living being next to me.

I kissed pillows. We had a support post in the middle of our basement living room. Alone, in that room, I would hug the post; it approximated the shape of a tall, thin man. I kissed it several times a week. Later, dark smudges formed on the white paint where my lips had been. No one asked how the smudges got there.

I remember one time I hugged Dad. I was eight or nine. Our family did not hug. I didn't know any family who hugged. The only person I hugged was Grandma Hager, because there was an unwritten rule that you could hug grandmas.

On this night, Dad got up from the couch and announced he was going to bed. I got up from my prone position in front of the television. "Wait," I said, and I walked to him. I put my arms around him and squashed my face into his soft belly. I heard Mom give a surprised laugh. Dad laughed a little, too, and patted my back awkwardly.

I had broken the unwritten rule that said you didn't do anything or say anything to make people uncomfortable. On the surface, everything should remain a placid lake, the calm before the storm, the topsoil that hides the tumult of the worms underneath that change the landscape through their shifting and tunneling through dirt. I never hugged Dad again. And now, newly on my own three years after his death, my craving for touch was strong.

Studies have shown that times of grief can result in incredible bonding between two people. One Internet message board asked people: Where is the best place to flirt? Number five on the list: funerals. The depth of sadness and loss dredges up other emotions, too—the desire to share, to offset the low with a high. Coldness replaced by warmth. The dead replaced by something living, very living, vibrant and real.

Dad died in 1990. Andy got married in 1992, Mom got married in 1993, and I got married in 1994. I was nineteen. We buried our former selves by joining others. Funeral bells and wedding bells sound the same.

I MET DAVID in the spring of my senior year of high school. My friends and I had joined a community drum line, even though we didn't play drums. We thought it would be a great way to meet cute guys. At the first practice, the director put cymbals in our hands, and we scanned the small group for potential mates, like deer in rutting season.

I spotted David. He was slim and slight, with blond hair. He was in college, played guitar, and wrote sensitive lyrics. We shared long talks on bus rides and around campfires that summer. By September, still on my own in Minneapolis but now enrolled in college, I had broken up with the boyfriend

Mom hated, and David had ended it with his longtime girl-friend who had been already picking out wedding dresses. We were a couple.

David lived with his parents. I spent my first weekend away from school tucked cozy under covers in his parents' spare bed-room. Mom had married a few weeks before, moved to Minne-apolis, and sold our Waseca house. Just in time I had found a family, a place to go, a home. I would cling tight to it and never leave.

His family enthralled me: a mom, a dad, and two sisters. His older sister spent most of her spare time bringing her husband and kids to the house. His younger sister was about my age and also lived at home; her boyfriend spent almost as much time at the house as I did. There was an aunt and uncle next door, and a storybook grandma who presided over everyone. The home reminded me of something out of *The Waltons*. The house was filled with energy and life, laughs, stories. There were no se-crets here, and everyone knew each other's business.

As David and I quickly grew closer, I spent every weekend at his house. I let the family subsume me. I gave myself to them, let myself become an adopted daughter. Even David's dad reminded me much of my own: easy-going, relaxed, loqua-cious. *How's my Rachael?* he'd say upon seeing me, and my heart melted. This was where I wanted to be; this was where I belonged. What were the chances I'd find this again? I'd been so lucky twice: first with my own family, and now with this one. David was a truly good guy—I could tell by the way he treated his mother, by the way he adored her. So in January, four months after we started dating, we got engaged.

Shortly before my wedding, my friend Diane saw Andy at a Waseca bar. By then, his short-lived marriage was over. That I was just nineteen and getting married was the talk among all my friends. In high school, I had been a budding feminist, chafing at any mention of husbands and children and picket fences. I was going to be a journalism star; I was going to make a name for myself. At the bar, Diane and Andy talked about me, how I was so young, how it couldn't possibly last.

Do you think you would have gotten married so soon if your dad hadn't died? Diane asked Andy.

No doubt I wouldn't have, he said. *That's exactly why I did it.*

At my wedding, I effectively buried Rachael Hager. I chose to take the Hanel name, creating even more distance from the girl I had been. The name of that girl now seems strange and unreal. It's like the name on a gravestone, the name of a person I know only by a string of letters or by stories about her told by others.

I wonder if Dad looked at the name Paul Hager and questioned who that person was. He had had to reinvent himself, too, to create a safe distance from everyday loss. Dad did not want to become an Icarus, flying too close to the emotions of death, only to get burned by despair. I didn't want to get too close to the burning brightness that was Rachael Hager—her memories, her grief, her family. That intensity held too much sorrow, too much longing for a life that no longer was. Staying with her would have been my downfall.

I SPENT YEARS thinking I should have grieved differently. Where are the fireworks, the bang, the reality-show cliffhanger? Even in writing this, I struggle in knowing I won't deliver the ending bombshell that the story seems to be leading to. There's no blowup with Mom. I didn't become estranged from my family, filled with bitterness. I didn't turn to drugs or wild sex to drown my grief.

But there's a distance between us, formed the night Dad died. I can still clearly hear the sound of doors shutting. And when I see Andy, maybe two, three times a year, even though he lives just thirty miles away, I picture him walking away down the stairs, legs, body, then head disappearing. We all started to separate that night, like bubbles that float out from one wand, born of one breath.

We confronted grief much as we confronted work. Grief was just another thing to do well, to control and perfect. Much as Dad approached the digging of a grave, or the way Uncle Ray methodically harvested his corn and soybeans, working late into a full-moon night until the job was done. Grief could be contained, like the steers that Grandpa kept in a pen by the barn. Grief could be domesticated, like dogs. Human nature wants to tame the wild. I could tame my grief by writing words on the page, acting, and collapsing into the arms of another.

ON MY BIRTHDAY, sometime in my late twenties, I met Mom for lunch at a suburban restaurant. As we were leaving, she said, "I have some things for you in the car." I waited by her black Cadillac as she rummaged in the backseat. She handed me a birthday card with twenty dollars inside. She also passed to me a fresh home-baked cake—marble with white frosting, my favorite. I put this in my car nearby.

"I have some other stuff, too," she said. She handed me a box with all of our old family photo albums inside, the photos I had pored over obsessively as a kid: the red photo album with Grandpa Hager's funeral photos in the back; the photo album with trees embossed on the front, full of Polaroids from our 1979 trip to North Dakota to visit the graves of my great-grandparents; the thick brown album documenting our lives from the late 1980s—our trip to the Black Hills, Renee's wedding.

"Wow. Thanks," I said, leafing through the albums. It's all I could think to say in my surprise. I didn't think to ask *Why are you giving them to me?* She gave them to me, not Renee, not Andy. Perhaps she sensed that I was the designated keeper of stories, that I always had been and always will be.

On the drive home, I wondered if I would be able to do the same thing that Mom just did. If David died and I remarried, what would I do with our family photos? What would I do with the photos that provided evidence that our lives together had existed? Without the photos, all we have are memories, and we know how quickly those can fade. I couldn't help but think of the word "erasure." Is that what Mom was doing? Can you erase a portion of a life without erasing all of it? I wasn't sure she could effectively put Dad away without her children fading as well. Maybe it was her way of taming grief. Shedding the old, all of it, to make way for a new marriage, a new house, a new life.

Another year, she gave me her wedding photos. Without fanfare, without a hint of sadness or longing, Mom brought the small, hand-sized mother's album that had belonged to Grandma Zimny. The former pearl-white cover was now grimy and yellowed with age, but the pictures inside were in pristine condition; many I had never seen before. The pictures provided many views of St. Mary's church, simple and white, a church that would be torn down fourteen years later. You can go to that spot now, on top of a hill, and look at the church bell that rang on their wedding day, housed in a tiny shelter. A memorial.

This was a wordless exchange, a piece from the past transcending time and space. But what was left unsaid rang loudly. *I don't need these anymore. That woman, that fresh-faced nineteen-year-old standing at an altar in a church that no longer exists, was unique to a place and time that has passed.*

* * *

IN A FARMHOUSE SOUTH OF WASECA, MINNESOTA, my mother's mother settles into a chair at her Formica-topped, steel-legged kitchen table, newspaper spread out before her. She has just finished washing lunch dishes that had been dirtied by cuts of beef between two pieces of bread, drizzled with thick gravy. The meal was followed by a homemade doughnut and coffee to wash it down—every meal must end with something sweet. Everything is clean; the house is quiet. Grandpa is outside, maybe in the barn, cleaning, feeding the steers and chickens, filling water troughs. Grandma's cup steams, the coffee as black as her hair. She's in her sixties, but her hair is still naturally Irish black, hardly a gray to be found. It's the black hair of her mom, the black hair of her brothers and sisters. Blessed with good genes, they are. Mom has the hair, Renee has the hair. But I have Dad's sandy brown mess; his is already growing gray, even in his thirties.

Grandma sips the coffee and peers through her glasses at the small print of the newspaper. Chin up, eyes down, until the words come into focus. No word of this *Waseca Journal* will go unread. Across the table, next to the scissors, sits a folded *Mapleton Messenger* that came in the morning's mail. Those words will not go unread, either. Grandma and Grandpa haven't lived near Mapleton for thirty years, back before they bought this farm. But Mapleton isn't far away, just forty miles, and familiar names still pop out in black ink. So month after month, Grandma keeps writing a check for the *Messenger,* a few dollars a year.

The newspapers are her lifeline to the outside world, just as Mom peers into different worlds through her books, and I peer into different worlds in the cemeteries. Grandma spends most days on the farm, only leaving to run errands in town, to drive her grandchildren to school or band practice, or to attend Mass on Sundays. Here, in newsprint, is proof that life exists beyond this small plot of land, beyond Grandpa, beyond her children and grandchildren. The newspapers can't replace her beloved old party-line telephone, where she listened silently as neighbors talked about finances, family troubles, who was born, died, and got married. But they will suffice.

In the *Waseca Journal*, news comes from Alma City, Otisco, Janesville. Grandma runs her index finger down the columns and spots names of neighbors and relatives—Holmes, Conway, Harguth, Stencel. When she spots a name she knows, the scissors that have been resting next to her spring into action. She brings the shears to the paper and cuts, slowly, her edges straight and neat.

Mostly she clips obituaries. She stops, takes time to read the short recounting of the person's life and list of survivors. She buys sympathy cards by the pack, the generic type with religious overtones: *We're praying for you during this difficult time.* She's sending more of those these days. She and Grandpa are growing older. People they once knew well, people they grew up with, are dying. Each snip, snip, snip of the sharp scissors blades brings her one moment closer to her own death. But still she clips, she preserves. As long as they exist in print, as long as they live in between the pages of her scrapbook, they aren't really dead.

She tucks these obits in with the others, much as she would tuck a child into bed. Her scrapbook is loose, messy. Grandma doesn't do anything special with the clips—doesn't laminate them, doesn't glue them in, doesn't arrange them in any particular order. Weddings, engagements, and birth announcements rest side by side with the obits.

Still, there's a pattern. Many of the dead are young. Many died unexpectedly. Mrs. Fred Gertz, sixty-one, open-heart surgery. Stanley Koziolek, sixty-four, heart attack. Duane Anderson, fifty, short illness. Harold Woitas, forty-seven, brief illness. In the 1970s, a heart attack is nearly always a death sentence. So many young and dead, so many young and alive left behind.

In Grandma's scrapbook, the world of the living meets the world of the dead. It's a "thin space," a notion from the tribe of ancient Celts from which she descended. In these thin spaces, a person can reach out and almost touch what's on the other side, whether it be God, angels, or the dead. Names and faces live on. The tiny stories in the scrapbook provide a portal.

Grandma isn't ready to throw these relatives and neighbors away, to crumple them up and throw them in the trash alongside the mundane news. The clipping and the snipping each day abate her greatest fear—that she, too, will fade into oblivion after death, that no one will remember her, no one will think of her time on earth, no one will speak her story. Three of her five children live, and they've married and have children of their own. But what about the day they are no longer here, the day her grandchildren are no longer here, and no one is left to remember? But if she exists in a clipping, a picture, a story, then she's still here.

The clippings remind her that life is beautiful and precious and unpredictable and that everyone shares grief. More than keeping the dead alive and on her tongue, the stories remind her that she's not alone. She's not the only mother in the world to deliver a dead baby. She's not the only one to bury the child in an unmarked cemetery plot. She's not the only mother to watch a doctor diagnose an adult son with leukemia, stay with the son during treatments, and watch the son's body shrink into itself and die.

Yet Mom gets her silence from somewhere. It filters downs, just as surely as the genes for black hair. Grandma doesn't talk about her baby. She doesn't talk about Norbert. They don't live in her scrapbook. She keeps the stories of others alive, but not her own.

There are other clippings besides obits. There are weddings and engagements and anniversaries. There are stories about neighbors, funny candid pictures of little kids. There are stories about priests and even a signed photo from a priest, collected as one would collect movie-star autographs.

Grandma's scrapbook holds beginnings, too. These don't negate the endings but rather bring everything around full circle. The alpha and omega, Genesis and Revelation, the Our Father at the beginning of the rosary and the Hail Holy Queen at the end. From my very beginning, I'm placed next to the dead: "Nov. 12, girl, to Mr. and Mrs. Paul Hager."

GRANDMA'S SCRAPBOOK lived on beyond her. Pancreatic cancer took her in 1978, the year I turned four. Grandpa kept many of her things: some clothes and her bright, sparkly costume jewelry in a black box embossed with gold stars. He kept the scrapbooks, too. I found them when Mom and I cleaned out his house after he died in 1992. The scrapbooks were sitting high on a closet shelf. I wonder if he ever touched them, brought them down, flipped through them, touched the tiny mementoes of people who had gone before, people he and Grandma both knew.

I brought them home. Mom, her brother, and her sister divided anything of worth, which was not much. The farming poor don't have crystal heirlooms or gilded teacups. I could not think of anything I wanted from that house, save for the scrapbooks. I was seventeen; I couldn't articulate their value. My heart didn't stop at the sight of them. But something seemed to speak from the books, telling me to bring them home and put them in my own closet. Something seemed to tell me that I would need them years later.

IN COLLEGE, I carried on the family tradition of making money off death. I earned six dollars an hour typing obituaries at the *Mankato Free Press*. The first day on the job, I walked into the front door of the *Free Press* and ascended the stairs to the second-floor newsroom that smelled of newsprint, ink, and coffee. I had heard stories all my life and read them, but until this point I had not known they could have a distinctive scent. Reporters' desks were cluttered with papers, files, and pens. Phones rang, people chattered, keyboards clicked. All those years of drinking in stories and here was a place that revolved around story. I didn't want to leave.

I met P.J., the tall news clerk with dark hair who would train me in my new duties. He let me sit at his desk, and he pulled another chair alongside me.

"I already saved some obituaries for you to start on. Here you go," he said, handing me the small stack of papers.

I grabbed the first one and looked at the name. Agnes Armstrong. Little Agnes Armstrong, the Irish dynamo with curly white hair who attended St. Joseph's church in Waldorf with my family.

"Oh, no," I said to P.J., "that's my best friend's grandma!"

Other grandmas filtered in over the years—ones I didn't know and ones I knew. I typed Grandma Hager's obituary and the obituary for David's grandma. I typed obituaries for my aunts and uncles. As I moved into the *Free Press* ranks as a reporter and copy editor, I carefully proofread obits for relatives or friends. They liked that I paid special attention to the words that would make it into print for all to see.

As a reporter, I chronicled the stories of others: the World War II veteran, the woman brainwashed by a 1970s cult, the Bosnian immigrant family. It wasn't the big-time journalism career I had once dreamed of, but it seemed fated. I felt compelled to write stories, etching words in newsprint much as words are etched into gravestones for the historical record. It didn't seem right that people should just disappear. I would write everyone's story if I could.

I FIND MYSELF CLIPPING OBITS. Snip, snip, snip. The lives are too important to toss out with the rest of the mundane news. I mostly clip obits of people I know, but I save the ones that tell a good story, too. The *Free Press* carries the obits of people who once lived in Waseca. And like Grandma, I write subscription checks to my hometown newspaper, even though I've been away nearly twenty years. The desire to clip, the desire for home, seems to be another thing imprinted on my DNA.

I press the obits into photo albums. Aunts, uncles, shoestring relatives, parents of friends, strangers. I don't often go back to them, which leads me to question why I even save them. I don't often go back to Dad's gravestone, either, but there's a certain comfort in knowing it's there, this proof that he existed. To preserve names and history, in paper or on stone, is what separates us from the animals.

But every year or so, I flip through Grandma's scrapbook. The scrapbook is like a mind map, evidence of how Grandma thought and what she considered important. I barely knew Grandma. I like having something she touched, thought about, saved. Something that Grandpa kept for a reason. Something I spirited out of her house, for reasons unknown to me at the time.

I thought I would end up far away from my hometown, but here I am, just thirty miles away. Once, long ago, I made plans to escape. Pig farmers and overalls and the smell of manure that wafted into our house did not scream sophistication. I thought I would fit in Minneapolis, but I was wrong. In the city, I was like a transplanted organ that works well for a while but ends up being rejected by the body.

My current town is so small that in the summer I can leave my front door, take a left from my driveway, and in two blocks, if I keep going straight, the tall cornstalks would subsume me. I could disappear like a shadow into them. If I drive just a half hour from my home, I can see the fields that Grandpa tended; I can be in the cemeteries where Dad dug graves. Their spirits linger there, and I'm reluctant to leave.

David and I sometimes talk of moving away. The beauty and cool and adventure of Lake Superior's North Shore call us, we who have never lived anywhere else except the farm prairie. But even now, even in the preliminary stages of planning to move—stages so early we can't even say for sure it's going to happen—I know what I would long for if we went away. I would long for the soil—the soil in which my grandfathers worked, in which my father worked. I would miss the dirt more than anything. I feel the pull, like people afflicted with geophagy, the desire to eat earth. I don't want to eat it, but I do want to ingest it, to have it live within me. I want dirt molecules to rise up and sink into my bones, to become part of my very being, just as with Grandpa and Dad. They worked in the dirt until their last days. They could not have done anything else and been happy. Tearing them away from the dirt would have killed a part of them.

* * *

ON MAGICAL SPRING DAYS I clip my feet into bicycle pedals and cruise along country roads. The steep hills rising up and out of the many nearby rivers and creeks make my heart want to pound out of my chest. Little-used country roads connect tiny towns, arteries to hearts. I head east, and in thirty minutes, I'm in Elysian. Who was the European settler who named this place? A farmer who knew the works of Virgil and Dante, someone who thought southern Minnesota evoked the essence of heaven.

Elysian looks like any other small Minnesota town: a gas station at the city limits, an aging water tower, faded red granaries. As I head out of the town, I hug the many fields and watch tractors prep for planting. The farmers massage the soil, getting it ready to bring forth life. I easily outrace the tractors, which plod along as I hit a high gear. I crank, crank, crank, lean and swift, the farmer heavy and slow.

I wave to each farmer. I usually do not have to wave first. In their fields, in their cabs, they welcome the sight of me, someone as eager to be outdoors in the spring air as they are. They raise a hand. No vigorous wave like that of an excited child, no slow back-and-forth like from a beauty queen. Just a raised hand, the white flesh of wrist and fingers poking out of a blue denim long sleeve. Sometimes, in true farmer fashion, just a raised index finger. It's a simple salute. If hands could speak, theirs would drawl *howzit goin'*—not a question, but a statement, the second word landing lower than the first. *Howzit goin'*. A placid, serene surface. I could be waving to Grandpa, waving to Dad.

I breathe in the freshly turned soil, and this is all I want to breathe, night and day. What strikes me is how sharply metallic the black earth smells. Like blood. Whenever I accidentally cut my finger and put my tongue to the wound, the metal taste surprises me. The rich red suggests I will taste something sweet, a cherry lollipop or licorice, but instead I taste the bland, cold gray of iron. It doesn't surprise me that blood and soil might taste the same, smell the same. They both sustain my life.

> I had about everything I wanted in life. A good family, a good
> farm, a good future. But the Lord gave it to me, and it was His
> to take away. (Jim Zimmerman)

DEEP IN GRANDMA'S SCRAPBOOK, amid the obituaries, Jim Zimmerman smiles from a faded, yellowed newspaper clip. It's 1961, two years after his family was killed. In the photo, a trim, tiny woman named Vivian stands next to him. They're at an altar; it's their wedding day. They met when Vivian's aunt read about Jim's tragedy in *Catholic Digest* and wrote to him on her niece's behalf. You see, Vivian was a widow. Her husband died of cancer.

In the photo, next to Jim and Vivian, stand Vivian's six young children.

I thought of Jim often, even after Dad died and I had no reason to go to Calvary Cemetery anymore. I thought of him when I crossed the railroad tracks by Sacred Heart, thought of him on my way to Owatonna when I passed his house on Highway 14. He flicked in and out of my consciousness, always on the periphery of my vision. Just as I had grabbed Grandma's scrapbooks without knowing why, I had studied the Zimmerman gravestone and tucked away Jim's story, somehow intuiting that I would draw on him later.

In *The Hero with a Thousand Faces,* the writer Joseph Campbell articulated what he called "the hero's journey," the narrative to which so many stories throughout time have adhered. Campbell summarizes the journey in his introduction: "A hero ventures forth from the world of common day into a region of supernatural wonder: fabulous forces are there encountered and a decisive victory is won: the hero comes back from this mysterious adventure with the power to bestow boons on his fellow man."

But a hero on her own has little hope. On their journeys, heroes are aided by mentors—people who show the hero the ways of the world and the keys to survival. In my own journey, mentors handed me clues to unlock secrets. According to some interpretations of Campbell's work, the mentor represents what the hero hopes to become. I gladly claim Jim Zimmerman as a mentor as well as my grandparents and Dad and Mom. They are mentors who have faced grief squarely and said *I will not succumb.*

My New Age phase didn't last. The answers I sought were within me all along. In *The Wizard of Oz,* Dorothy's intellect, heart, and courage were always within her—it just took a mentor to point that out. My mentors pointed to words on gravestones and in scrapbooks. My answers were in prayer, in rosary beads, in church—namely, the fourth row from the front, left side.

I RETURNED TO CALVARY CEMETERY on a sunny late August day in 2006. Joe Harguth, my best friend's dad, died in a motorcycle accident, and mourners gathered around the small hole where his ashes would rest. This section was now peppered with gravestones; twenty years ago, when I was riding my bike around here, it was open space.

After the priest talked, and my friend Angie leaned into her mother's shoulder, and everyone else walked back to their cars and left for the funeral luncheon, I settled into the passenger seat of my friend Diane's car.

"Drive around back," I said. "If Andy's back there, we can say 'hi.'" My brother had taken over Dad's grave-digging business. Diane pulled away slowly, and when the other cars turned to exit the cemetery gates, she took a left and led us deeper into Calvary. I looked for Andy's truck in the trees, where he and his shovels would be hiding from view.

I didn't see Andy, but I saw Jim Zimmerman.

He had been at Joe's graveside with us, paying his respects to the man he knew from the Waseca farming community and as a fellow Sacred Heart parishioner. When the rest of us had headed to our cars, Jim had walked slowly through the grass, his gait stiff but steady, back hunched into the familiar curve of a seasoned farmer. He crossed the gravel road and passed tombstones until he stood at the graves of his first wife and children, and his second wife.

I craned my neck toward him and watched through the car window. He looked so small, so old now, nearing eighty. He clasped his hands in front of him, bowed his bald head, and faced the gravestone.

I didn't want to watch him for long, didn't want to disturb this private moment. Yet I didn't want to look away. We drove past, and I turned in the seat and watched him until I could see him no longer.

Baby grave in Glenwood Cemetery, Mankato, Minnesota

Chapter 13

WHAT WAS LEFT BEHIND

*D*AD PARKS THE PICKUP in the old part of Woodville. He and I will start here, where the job is easy. It is mid-June, and rainbows of flowers left over from Memorial Day, drops of blues, reds, and yellows, puncture the green landscape. Fake carnations, fake roses, fake petunias; flowers molded into the shape of crosses, circles, squares; flowers arranged into the words "Mom" or "Dad." They all need to go.

These arrangements make it hard for Dad to trim around gravestones. He has to cast a wide berth lest he inadvertently lop off a faux bloom and anger a family if they visit and see what he has done. But in those couple of weeks after Memorial Day, grass grows in tall patches around tombstones where his trimmer can't reach. This drives him crazy. The sign at the front gate states that all flowers have to be removed by June 15. We arrive the morning of June 16 to throw away any that remain.

Dad assigns this job to me. At our small cemeteries, I can do this by myself, walking the short distance between gravestones and Dad's pickup, where I toss flowers into the back for later disposal. But Woodville is too big; I need help. So after Dad finishes trimming, while Mom and Andy continue to mow, he works alongside me.

Where we start, wide trees with thick trunks loom, oaks with craggy branches that stamp out the sun. Grass grows here in fits and spurts, blades scattered randomly, wispy hairs on a balding man's head. Flowers are just as sparse. The dates on the stones range from mid- to late 1800s. Few of these dead would have family around here anymore, forgotten even on Memorial Day.

Dad and I move down row after row, bending to pull arrangements out of the earth. Clumps of dirt cling to plastic serrated stems. I give each one a shake, and dirt crumbles away. These arrangements are ugly. A few weeks before, they had been on sale for a buck or two in the aisles of Waseca's Ben Franklin store. The sun and wind and rain have cracked the thick plastic leaves and flowers like winter weather dries skin. If I ever have to leave flowers at a grave, I think, I would never leave flowers like this. My arms overflowing with junk, I walk to the back of the pickup and toss them in. When the pickup can't hold any more, Dad packs the flowers down with his hand to keep them from spilling over the sides, I hop in the passenger side, and we motor down to the dirt piles next to Woodville's garage. Dad backs up the truck to the dirt. I get out of the cab, walk to the back, and hoist myself into the truck bed. With my hands and feet, I shove the flowers toward Dad. He grabs armfuls of arrangements and throws them onto the mounds of excess dirt he had hauled there, leftover from graves. I step down and survey the fake flowers blooming from the dirt. One arrangement catches my eye. It's pristine and out of place, the flowers silky and blue. Lace cups the blooms and light blue ribbons curl down and around the stem. Blue is my favorite color.

I reach up to save it from burial. I touch the petals—soft fabric instead of cheap plastic. This one is going home with me. It will be the perfect bridal bouquet for when I play wedding, *step—pause—opposite foot forward—step—pause—opposite foot forward,* down our narrow hallway, back and forth in front of my bedroom, a sheet pinned to my hair like a veil.

We drive back and park near the "can" section, the section with the outhouse. Dad had named each section in Woodville. That made it easier to plan the day, to tell Mom and Andy where to mow. In the evening, at the supper table, Dad might say "Let's start with the old section tomorrow" or the "wet section" or the "Rethwill section," so named because of the big gravestone etched with the last name of my dentist.

Dad and I work the can section. There are more flowers here, since the gravestones are newer than in the old section. At a gravestone with an elaborate arrangement wired tightly to the front, I pause. Clearly, whoever put it there wanted it to stay, so I move on.

Dad sees me. "Whaddya doin'?" he asks. "What about those flowers?" He jerks his thumb toward the arrangement I had just ignored.

I shrug. "But it's wired on there."

He shakes his head. "That don't matter. Take it anyway. They all have to go."

So I pull and tug, move the wires up one end of the gravestone, then the other, finally wiggling the entire thing up and off.

After the can section, we walk across Woodville's narrow blacktop road to the "long" section. This section runs nearly the entire length of Woodville, widening and narrowing at different points. In this section, underneath the shade of tall elms, lie the babies.

* * *

I DO NOT HAVE CHILDREN. I've been married since 1994. My ovaries work as far as I know, and my husband's sperm likely swim just fine. I'm among the voluntary childless. According to the Census Bureau, 13.2 percent of white women my age who are married do not have children. Among women like me—white, late thirties, married, master's degree—15.7 percent are childless, roughly one out of seven. But how many women are childless by choice? The numbers don't probe that deeply into the psyche.

I desire to make my world as small as possible. Curl it up into a little ball, so small I can hold it in the palm of my hand. Dad's death rocked his wide, wide world, a world huge with family and friends.

When I think of having children, two major fears stop me. One, that I would leave them behind in the way Dad left me, causing them grief and sadness. In the natural world, this is how it works: children outlive parents. But the other fear, perhaps even stronger, is that I might lose a child. I would be so fearful of something dreadful befalling my child that I would become everything I despise in parents—hovering, smothering, protective. I would want to be with my child at all times, to watch, to ensure his safety, his breathing, his being. I would never rest because of the vigilant watching. Every time I let my child go—to school, to a friend's house, to an overnight camp—would feel like a little death. I would see danger in every grape, playground, window shade, fever. In every crib, car, tricycle, bicycle. In every storm, strange dog, forest. I fear that the death of someone young and innocent, a being entrusted into my care, would be the death that after all these years would plunge me into darkness.

Rationally, I know I would survive. But I don't want to take the chance. If I don't have children, then I have nothing to lose. As strong as I've been in the face of death, it's a mask. I'm not strong at all. I was given one deep well of strength to draw on, and I ran it dry after Dad died. I had no concept of rationing, so I suspect I have nothing left.

I have never spoken these reasons out loud. People ask, of course. It's one of the first questions upon meeting someone new: "So, do you guys have kids?" David and I shake our heads, answer with a simple no. Most people leave it at that, though I can see their *Why not?* like a thought bubble hovering above their heads, going through all the problems and obstacles that would explain our answer: She's infertile. He's infertile. Her choice. His choice. Sexual dysfunction. One of them is secretly gay and they don't even have sex. I wonder how often people give legitimate weight to the idea I'm childless by choice.

Closer friends probe more deeply. I get away with saying, "We just don't want kids. We like the ability to do anything, go anywhere, at anytime." It's the truth. But so are the baby graves.

AT PILGRIM'S REST CEMETERY outside of Mankato there is an unmarked grave. The cemetery is home to the Hanels and the Manskes, David's relatives. He doesn't have to traipse around to numerous cemeteries, as I do, to find his relatives. They are located compactly in this one spot.

The unmarked grave is his brother, Michael. He died as an infant five years before David was born. We stop at the cemetery each Memorial Day with his parents. Marlene walks with purpose over to the grave. She points out the location for us. Without her, we can't find it. Someday she'll be gone and Michael will be gone, too, lost to buried memories.

At the grave, we hear the story again. Healthy baby came home from the hospital in 1966, but a few days later, he was blue and dead in the crib. David's birth was a godsend, a second chance to raise a precious boy. David remained Marlene's only boy, and you will not witness a greater love of a mother for her son.

She had a marker made for Michael in the days after his burial. A relative owned a funeral home and made a temporary marker. But someone at the cemetery didn't like it. The exact story isn't clear, muddied over time, but perhaps he thought it was cheap and tacky, and he wanted uniformity among granite markers. In disgust and rage, amid sadness, Marlene yanked out the marker and never put one back.

Every season that goes by, each time new leaves form and then fall, the memories fade a bit more. Without a gravestone, this once-living being will soon not be remembered. But it might be Marlene's way of protecting herself. She thinks of Michael every day. In her darkest moments, does she try to convince herself it was a dream? Without a marker, with just a blank expanse of grass to gaze on, it could be just a dream.

WOODVILLE IS THE ONLY CEMETERY Dad and I work in with a section just for babies. It's not marked as such with a sign or archway. No arrows point you there. But you know. You know by the sudden pattern of flat, tiny markers that break the landscape of knee-high granite tombstones. You know by pinwheels blurring whirls of primary colors in the wind. You know by the lamb statues that anchor a corner of a stone. You know by toys left there, teddy bears and dolls and cars. You know by balloons tethered to wooden posts stuck in the ground. The markers of a couple of dozen babies lie here, filtering in and around a few bigger gravestones of adults that form a sort of protectorate, ersatz aunts and uncles and grandparents who keep watch.

The babies bear the last names of my classmates—Bartz, Dahnert, Wabner. I don't know if these babies are actually related to classmates, but in this small town, I am sure in some way they are. These siblings will always be babies, stuck in time, while the rest of us grow older.

I'm not much older than some of these children when they died, and their trinkets appeal to me. I could take home a balloon, or a teddy bear, maybe put it in my room. I reach down to grab a pinwheel out of the ground, but I hesitate. Something seems wrong about taking from the babies. But Dad's words echo in my head: "They all have to go." I continue my reach. Dad turns around and sees me. He's quick to speak.

"Don't take anything from the baby graves. Just leave it."

I straighten up and look at him. His eyes meet mine; he shakes his head. I understand that here he will go slowly with the trimmer. He will take the time to pause, bend down, move the toys and flowers, trim, pause again, and move them back.

I LOVED DOLLS AS MUCH AS ANY GIRL. I had a good collection of babies, most of them hand-me-downs from Renee. Babies with soft plastic faces, fabric bodies, coarse hair. My favorite floppy-bodied baby had a bit-off nose. Whether it was myself or Renee who bit it off, I do not know. But I could see the appeal in gnawing the rubbery mold, comforting like a pacifier.

I swaddled my babies and fed them bottles with the "milk" inside dried up and long gone. I cradled them in my arms, rocked them, put them to bed. My favorite part was holding them. I would just sit with them in my arms. My arms seemed to naturally form a crook, a resting place for a baby's weak head.

I constantly formed baby names in my head. I was so obsessed with names that I ordered a baby name book from one of our school book fairs when I was ten or eleven. I went through a "J" phase—Juanita, Jacqueline, Joseph. Then I moved on to the classics. For many years, I thought my girls would be named Grace Kelly (a nod to the iconic actress) and Elizabeth Ann (Ann for Grandma Hager). Family factored heavily into the names of my future boys: Gregory Edward (after a grandpa and great-grandpa) and Paul (for Dad).

After Dad died, my desire for babies disappeared. I didn't know it then, of course. I didn't feel an invisible hand clench my uterus and make it cold. But I stopped thinking about baby names. I didn't crave to hold a child in my arms. My friend Jolene raved about babies. She cuddled her baby cousins and said how she could not wait to have a family. I didn't feel it anymore.

Studies have shown that mothers who lose a child experience very physical symptoms of grief and loss, more than the stereotypical heavy heart, sick stomach, and headaches. Researchers have reported that women actually feel as if their arms are missing in the absence of something to hold. "It feels like [the baby is] just snatched from you. And it's an incredible feeling, as if your arms have been chopped off," says one mother. Another mother reported that she found herself rocking. She was drawn to rocking chairs. Even standing, she found she habitually moved from the balls of her feet to her heels, swaying to an invisible rhythm.

IT WASN'T LONG BEFORE I KNEW A BABY AT WOODVILLE.

During my first-grade year, Ms. Morgan, a dark-haired, athletic third-grade teacher, would visit my teacher, Mr.

Schmidt, on lunch breaks and after school. My classmates and I somehow intuited that this was a courtship. It must have been their shared smiles, perhaps the way they touched each other on the arm. Maybe it was the way they sought each other out during school programs in the gym. In any case, my friends and I giggled and made smooching noises when they got together. Mr. Schmidt and Ms. Morgan rolled their eyes and laughed.

Ms. Morgan soon became Mrs. Schmidt. One year, her belly stretched wide and her gait shifted to an uncomfortable waddle. I was witness to the entire cycle—the courtship, the marriage, the pregnancy. All how it's supposed to be, in the order prescribed. But the baby section proved that parents could outlive children.

Dad buried Isabella Schmidt, who was stillborn, in a newer baby section a few yards away from the original one. She's next to the narrow cemetery blacktop road, near a few other babies who died in the late 1970s and early 1980s. Dad buried only a couple of babies each year. He dug the graves by hand, scooping out just a few shovelfuls of dirt. He didn't take any money.

I lingered at Isabella's grave each time I was at the baby section. There were always toys and balloons at her grave, and real flowers in a clay pot. I never actually saw the Schmidts there. But I imagined they held hands, held each other, while looking at the grave. I wondered if they took comfort that Isabella was near other children to keep her company. Did Mrs. Schmidt rock at the grave? Did she feel as if her arms were gone?

At Isabella's grave I prayed. I didn't use words. I closed my eyes and balled up my feelings, much as I would crumple a piece of scratch paper. With effort, I sent it out into the world, to the Schmidts.

I would reach down and touch the trinkets the Schmidts had left behind. If only I could have reached out to save Isabella, just as I could reach to pluck pretty flowers from the dirt, flowers that clearly didn't belong. Instead, I lifted my fingers to my lips, place my fingers on the gravestone, and walk away.

The family tree on the back of my parents' gravestone

EPILOGUE

$\mathscr{A}$UNT ROSANNE brought a few photo albums to the Hager family reunion. The big bunch of us reunites twice a year—once in the summer at Aunt Helen's and once for a Christmas lunch. Only three of Grandma's eight sons survive. Besides Davey, Neil, and Dad, Donnie and Louie are gone, victims of the Hager heart. Her six daughters remain strong—none has died since Lucille and Mary Jean in 1933. Cousin Nicky is gone, a motorcycle crash in 1998; and cousin Derek is gone, too, a heart attack at just twenty-four.

The photo albums sat unopened and untouched on a table in the garage across from the hot dish fashioned from scalloped potatoes and diced hot dogs, potato salad, and rhubarb bars. Some cousins chased their children; others greedily ate. I browsed the books in solitude.

One book was sorted by family, all of Dad's siblings and their offspring in birth order. The pictures spanned decades—black-and-whites mingled with the most current pictures. I flipped the pages, smiling at young aunts and uncles—Susie looking great in a bikini after birthing two kids, Gene in his army uniform.

I paused at my family and studied each picture carefully. I had seen most of the photographs over the years, but one was new. The laughter and chatter around me faded out, and tears sprang to my eyes. This picture is a candid shot at Rosanne and Wayne's house on Julie's ninth birthday. A professional photographer Rosanne was not; the mint-green wall of her dining room and the window's gold drapes overwhelm the photo. Julie's construction paper poinsettia and Santa Claus are still stuck to the wall with Scotch tape two weeks after Christmas. A macramé plant holder hangs in the window.

Four of us—Dad, Julie, my cousin Abe, and I—are at the bottom of the frame. I'm wearing the favorite outfit of my fifth year—a J. C. Penney green velvet jumper dress over a long-sleeved, white, high-collared shirt with a bow tied neatly at the neck. I had worn the dress to Christmas Eve midnight Mass at St. Joe's, then to Grandma Hager's the next evening for the boisterous family holiday. I wore it yet again to Wayne and Rosanne's farm for the birthday party.

Dad is wearing the best smile I've ever seen on him. He and Julie are in front of the two birthday cakes Mom made, one rectangular and one round. Dad is kneeling, which makes him even shorter than Julie. Julie's eyes are closed, but she's smiling. I'm grinning, too, Dad and I looking at the camera. We see only the back of Abe's blond head because he's watching the silliness.

What struck me as I looked at the picture, the feeling that hit the pit of my stomach, is how happy Dad looks. His smile is wide, pure. Why he's so happy, I don't know. He's being goofy, being Dad. He's kneeling at the table, pretending it's his birthday and all the fuss is for him. He's the only adult who got down on our level. We all think it's pretty funny. At that moment, I was proud to have such a funny dad. He was the dad who made people laugh, who made people happy.

I have many pictures of Dad, and he's smiling in most of them. But this picture of Rosanne's captures his very being perfectly, in a way I have not seen before. This one picture, this one moment in January 1980, sums up Dad's whole life.

Not only that, but now I have proof. I have proof that this is my dad. I can show this picture to people who never met him and say *See? Here's who he was. You want to know what he was like? Everything you need to know is in this picture.*

I took the picture and made copies. One is in a frame on my desk. An image, or a string of letters, is all it takes to start a story.

IT TOOK MANY YEARS before I learned that signs from the dead are much more subtle than I had expected back in high school. Back then, I closed the New Age books in frustration because Dad wouldn't come back to me in the way I wished, living and breathing at the foot of my bed. I dismissed the orange moon, heavy and full, that appeared the night of Dad's death. I didn't register the bald eagle that swooped in front of my car on the highway, even though it was where bald eagles normally do not appear. But finally, in dream after dream, I feel Dad. I see him, hear him, talk to him.

One dream stands out. I was back at the old house, the one in the country. Time had moved on; I was an adult, working the newspaper job I had in real life but living at home with Mom and Dad. I stood in the bathroom, the mirror and tub exactly as I remembered them. I dressed up quite a bit that day for work. I wore a skirt and even nylons, and took special care to apply my makeup. My hair was perfectly coiffed. In my dream, I was pretty in a way I had always longed to be, beautiful like Cheryl Tuttle.

I stepped out of the bathroom and into the hallway that led to the kitchen. Mom was working in the kitchen, baking or cooking something. From there I could see into the dining room, the layout exactly as I remembered. I saw the back of a head at the table, topped by sandy brown hair bleached by the sun.

"Is that Dad?" I wondered to myself. It couldn't be. I knew he was dead, that he shouldn't have been there. But it was him. There was no mistaking his hair, and I could see the blue collar of his work shirt. I smiled, and excitement tightened my stomach. I knew it had been a long time, yet Mom didn't act strangely. It was as if they had always been there, in that house, just waiting for me, waiting to come together as a family. Dad turned around to look at me and started to clap. I smiled a little out of surprise.

"Why are you clapping?" I asked him, embarrassed from the attention.

"You deserve to be appreciated more," he told me.

Then I woke up.

AT AN EARLY AGE, fairy tales created for me a world that could be. If I could write my own fairy tale, it might be something like this:

I drive down Interstate 35 on a Friday afternoon. I exit at Medford, drive past Resurrection Cemetery where Uncle Neil lies, and past Corpus Christi where the other Hagers are buried. On the Snake Trail toward Waseca, past Aunt Helen's house and the fancy houses on Clear Lake Drive. Out of Waseca, past the former Birds Eye plant, past Dad's ag school that's now a federal prison, past what used to be E. F. Johnson. I pass Calvary Cemetery and go over the Wilton Bridge. I pull into the gravel driveway on the farm, gravel crunching under my tires. It's David and I in the car; John and Renee, with Sean and Katie, are already there. Andy, too—it's my fairy tale, so he's a central part of this family, married with kids. It's Dad's birthday, or Mom's birthday, or Mother's Day, or some other excuse to all get together for the weekend. A lolling Friday night, then Saturday and most of Sunday in the country, a precious couple of days away from work and obligations and stress. A weekend back home in the quiet country, for this will always be home, no matter where I live. There are games—cribbage and Trivial Pursuit—and maybe we help Dad put together his latest five-thousand-piece jigsaw puzzle. Mom cooks, a rich meal of potatoes and meat and dessert, cake or cookies or a new creation of hers that will win grand prize at the Minnesota State Fair (that part is not fairy tale).

But we all know fairy tales aren't real. They are only places we go in our imaginations to escape the reality of our lives. They give us a respite where we can pause to let in beauty. A place where beauty will not die.

Instead of the fairy tale, here is what is: Mom and Renee and Andy and I revolve in our own orbits. We're in the same solar system, birthed of the same place, but only circling around each other—although I'm not sure this is really any different than it has always been. Even from my earliest days I felt alone, even when surrounded by family. Renee was out of the house when I was just eight years old; Andy was forever just a shadow. Mom would read a book in the other room, while Dad slept on the couch or went off to Happy Chef for some social time.

The time we do spend together seems like a formality, somewhat forced, not as easy as the frequent family get-togethers of the Hanels. We do Thanksgiving and Easter dinner, gathering at Mom's house in the northern metro suburbs for four, five hours at most. Andy's never there. At Christmas we get together on a Saturday afternoon before or after the holiday. Mom is considerate and courteous, giving all of us the chance to have the actual holiday with the families we married into. I badly want it to be different, but I've never said so. As the youngest, I've never felt it was my place to lead.

CHERYL AND DAWN TUTTLE lie one hundred yards to the west of Dad. To the east you can see Uncle Harold's grave, and Vicki is just to the south. On either side of Dad are two other men who died young and left children at home: John Trumbull and Paul Roesler. Just a year after Dad died, Brent Roesler, one year ahead of me in school, was killed in a car crash. Now he's buried next to his dad and my dad; the western sun has bleached Brent's photo on his gravestone.

Dad's gravestone is etched with the most words and images of any I've seen. On the front, the long poem of "Ideals," and the eagle, the backhoe, and the piano. On the back is the family tree that branches to my great-grandparents. Even if I weren't here to tell the story, Mom and Dad made sure that the story could tell itself.

ACKNOWLEDGMENTS

I am tremendously grateful for the organizations and people who have supported me along this journey. For monetary support, I thank the Prairie Lakes Regional Arts Council (with grants funded by the McKnight Foundation) and the Cornucopia Arts Center in Lanesboro, Minnesota. The Loft Literary Center in Minneapolis has provided me with countless educational and collaborative opportunities. I treasured my year in the Loft's mentorship program and appreciated the guidance from nonfiction mentors Elmaz Abinader and especially Barrie Jean Borich. My fellow mentees (Rebecca Kanner, Mai Neng Moua, and Margie Newman) helped me find my voice, and Jerod Santek ensured the smooth operation of it all. At the Loft, teaching artists Cheri Register and Elizabeth Jarrett Andrew have been instrumental in giving me feedback during my writing process.

Thanks to the editors of the following journals for publishing excerpts from this memoir: *New Delta Review, The Truth about the Fact, Ghoti,* and *Bellingham Review,* and *Stardust and Fate: The Blueroad Reader,* edited by my longtime teacher, mentor, and friend John Gaterud. John opened my eyes to the exciting form of creative nonfiction and its possibilities.

Thanks to Todd Orjala and all the staff at the University of Minnesota Press who have worked to get this book into print and beyond.

As a writer, I have a wonderful community of support. I thank the Sisters for their fine understanding of words and incredible insights on story. I admire Ann Rosenquist Fee's boundless creative energy and ideas; it's my hope that in simply being near her some will rub off onto me. I have enjoyed many car rides and class time with Lisa MB Simons. The writing and artistic talent in the Mankato community buoys me.

My sister, Renee Hilgren, and brother, Andy Hager, shared some of their recollections with me.

This is my story, although others may have different perspectives. I made every effort to capture the emotional truth of events. In a few instances I changed names to preserve privacy. Any errors are my own, and I apologize for any inadvertent pain that may arise from the telling.

I thank my mother, Loretta Ratajczyk, for gifting me a sense of story and reverence for the past. She created one of the best environments in which a child could grow and learn. I never doubted that I could be whatever I wanted to be.

To all whose stories appear in this book, especially Dad, my eternal thanks for shaping me into the person I have become.

Special thanks go to David, of course, for his immense patience, encouragement, and understanding. Everyone should be so lucky to have such a partner in life.

I have been incredibly blessed in my life, and I would be remiss in not thanking God, from whom all blessings flow.

RACHAEL HANEL is a writer, university administrator, and journalist. She has written more than twenty nonfiction books for children, and her essays have been published in the *Bellingham Review* and *New Delta Review*. She lives in Minnesota.